COMPASS AMERICAN GUIDES
An imprint of Fodor's Travel

YELLOWSTONE
and Grand Teton National Parks

BY BRIAN KEVIN · PHOTOGRAPHY BY JEFF VANUGA

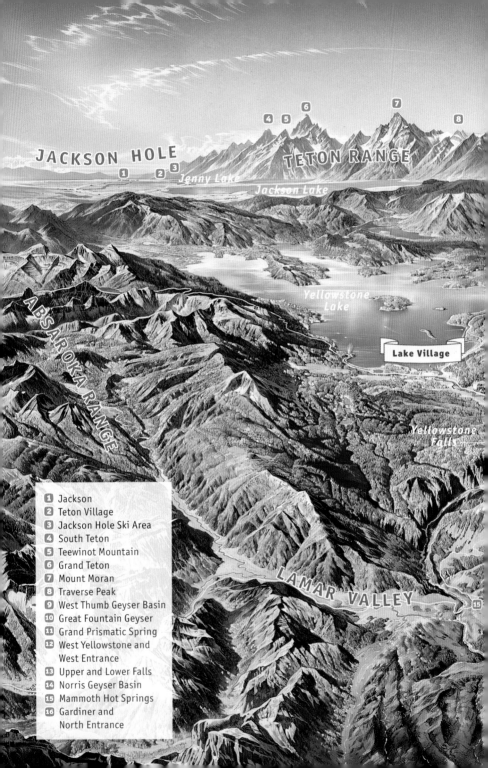

JACKSON HOLE

TETON RANGE

Jenny Lake

Jackson Lake

ABSAROKA RANGE

Yellowstone Lake

Lake Village

Yellowstone Falls

LAMAR VALLEY

1 Jackson
2 Teton Village
3 Jackson Hole Ski Area
4 South Teton
5 Teewinot Mountain
6 Grand Teton
7 Mount Moran
8 Traverse Peak
9 West Thumb Geyser Basin
10 Great Fountain Geyser
11 Grand Prismatic Spring
12 West Yellowstone and
   West Entrance
13 Upper and Lower Falls
14 Norris Geyser Basin
15 Mammoth Hot Springs
16 Gardiner and
   North Entrance

PANORAMA VIEW OF
YELLOWSTONE AND JACKSON
HOLE, LOOKING SOUTH

PITCHSTONE PLATEAU

Shoshone Lake

Grant Village

9

Old Faithful

10   11

Madison

12

13

14

Norris

Canyon Village

GALLATIN RANGE

15

16

BERANN

Bison warm themselves
at a thermal pool in
Yellowstone National Park.

Aspen trees in Bridger–Teton National Forest. Since aspens share one root system, a whole stand of trees will turn colors simultaneously in fall.

COMPASS AMERICAN GUIDES: Yellowstone and Grand Teton National Parks

COMPASS SENIOR EDITOR: Jennifer Paull
DESIGNERS: Tigist Getachew, Nora Rosansky, Chie Ushio
CREATIVE DIRECTOR: Fabrizio La Rocca
PRODUCTION EDITOR: Evangelos Vasilakis
PHOTO EDITOR: Melanie Marin
ILLUSTRATONS: William Wu
MAP DESIGN: Mark Stroud, Moon Street Cartography
PRODUCTION MANAGER: Angela L. McLean

COVER PHOTO: Buffalo in Grand Teton National Park, by Jeff Vanuga

First Edition

ISBN 978-1-4000-1935-9
ISSN 1943–0094

Compass American Guides, 1745 Broadway, New York, NY 10019

PRINTED IN CHINA
10 9 8 7 6 5 4 3 2

A petroglyph left by Greater Yellowstone's earliest inhabitants. ▶ ▶

Dedicated to my parents, who regularly unplugged the Nintendo and loaded me into a camper, and to Mel, my favorite adventure companion.

Contents

MAPS AND CHARTS

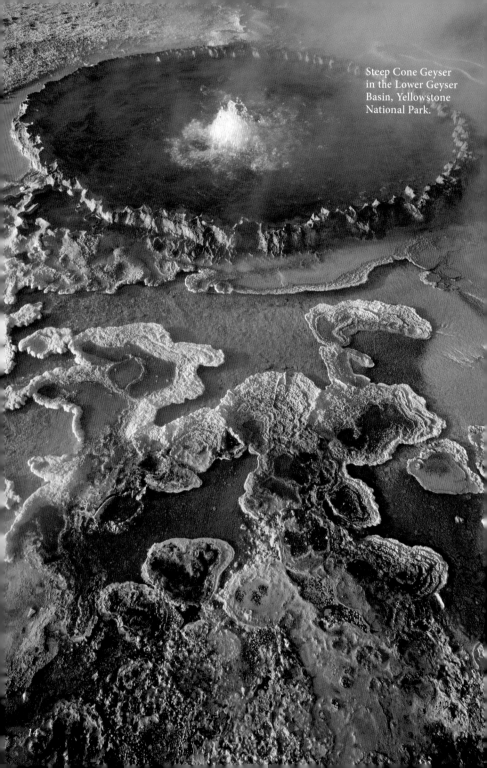

Steep Cone Geyser
in the Lower Geyser
Basin, Yellowstone
National Park.

14

Introduction

When I was a kid, my parents once drove me two hours to the Milwaukee Public Museum to see an exhibit called *Dinamation Dinosaurs.* I, like any red-blooded American seven-year-old, was deep in the throes of my dinosaur phase. *Dinamation Dinosaurs* was one of those newly popular animatronic exhibits, an "edutainment" display where giant robot brontosaurs grazed herky-jerky behind a velvet rope, sending kids with stegosaurus backpacks into paleo-pleptic spasms of glee as a voiceover explained the finer points of herbivore digestion.

Exhibits like this blew my mind, and the minds of hundreds of thousands of other kids, because they *did something.* Why stare at a pile of bones when we could watch T-Rexes the size of grain elevators swinging their tails, gnashing fiberglass teeth, and roaring ferocious, prerecorded roars? Children and adults alike fell for the moving parts. Museums and science centers quickly noticed this, and they've worked hard to incorporate everything from hands-on multimedia displays to Abe Lincoln androids.

So it's not surprising to anyone who has spent some time in Yellowstone National Park that occasionally a fellow visitor will sidle up to you at a hot spring, stare for a minute or two at the simmering water, and then ask, "Does this one *do anything*?"

It does, of course. When I hear this question, I'm tempted to answer, "Why yes! It simmers at something like 160 degrees Fahrenheit for 24 hours a day, 365 days a year. It circulates superheated water by convection through miles of subterranean fissures, dissolving and depositing ancient minerals along the way. It sustains entire colonies of microscopic bacteria—great, Technicolor mats of them—that thrive in temperatures no other organism on Earth can withstand."

I might want to answer this way, but I don't. I know that all the visitor really means is that he or she would like to see a geyser erupt. And that's understandable, because, let's face it, erupting geysers are incredible.

But I also don't answer this way because to do so would obscure a more important point: the wonders of Greater Yellowstone only amplify when you actively connect with them. This could mean lacing up your hiking boots and hitting some of the parks' 1,500 miles of trail. It might mean trying to wrap your brain around Ma Nature's geothermal hijinks with some help from an interpretive guide. The Yellowstone ecosystem has been quietly doing its thing for a few million years now. It's only when *you* do something to engage this landscape that you acquire the truest appreciation for the mountains, the hot springs, and the wildlife.

Yellowstone National Park is the country's original hands-on multimedia exhibit. It belches, thunders, and hisses. It shifts and quakes and burns. It teems with animals, from pikas to bison. When it was established in 1872, it introduced the world to the very concept of national parks, a model that Wallace Stegner famously hailed as "the best idea we ever had." Grand Teton joined the fold a few decades later, and together the two parks contain 4,000 square miles so chock-full of edutainment that a book like this one can only hope to scratch the surface.

I was well beyond my dinosaur phase when I first glimpsed Greater Yellowstone. As a college senior on summer break I hitchhiked into the park in the late 1990s, not expecting to see much more than a crowded tourist carnival and a handful of geysers. Instead I found an infinitely rich and varied landscape, one with more room to explore than a person could cover during a lifetime of summer breaks. I've since gone back to Yellowstone and Grand Teton national parks as a tourist, a backpacker, a seasonal employee, and an eager wannabe tour guide. Today I live just up the road in western Montana, near enough that I can make a few trips each year and sometimes show the place off to my houseguests.

And each time I pass through the entrance gates I still feel giddy and awed, like a seven-year-old at a dinosaur exhibit, gaping my way through a surreal space of nature, history, and wonder.

Brian Kevin

HOW TO USE THIS BOOK

This guide tackles the national parks in three main chapters. Yellowstone is divided into the Lower Loop (the southern part of the park, starting at Old Faithful) and Upper Loop (the northern part of the park), defined by the figure eight of the main park roads. The Grand Teton National Park chapter follows.

Each park chapter is divided into regions corresponding to park villages. Sights and activities described in each section are found in or within a half-hour's drive of those villages. Because long driving distances often separate dining options in the parks, you'll most likely find yourself eating wherever you're staying or passing through, so listings for restaurants are also included in these village-based regional sections.

All three park chapters highlight a few favorite hikes. These are listed in "sweat order," beginning with gentler strolls and working up to longer, more challenging excursions. Trailheads are readily identifiable unless otherwise noted.

The next chapter digs into the gateway towns, such as Jackson, hitting the best sights, places to eat, and town-based activities.

Finding a place to stay is best done in advance, and your location will strongly influence your park experience. For this reason, reviews of hotels, lodges, and campgrounds are organized by village or town in a single, browsable "Where to Stay" chapter. Both restaurants and accommodations are listed, using the following price categories, in descending order from most to least expensive.

RESTAURANTS
(average cost of a main course at dinner or the equivalent)

$$$$=over $25	$$$=$15-$25	$$=$10-$15	$=under $10

LODGING AND CAMPING
(a single night's peak-season rate for a standard double room)

$$$$=over $175	$$$=$100-$175	$$=$50-$100	$=under $50

Throughout the chapters, my recommendations for the best sights, activities, or places to stay and eat are indicated with a ★ icon. In the "Best Experiences" chapter that starts this guide, you'll find an at-a-glance roundup of my personal favorites and those of the photographer, Jeff Vanuga.

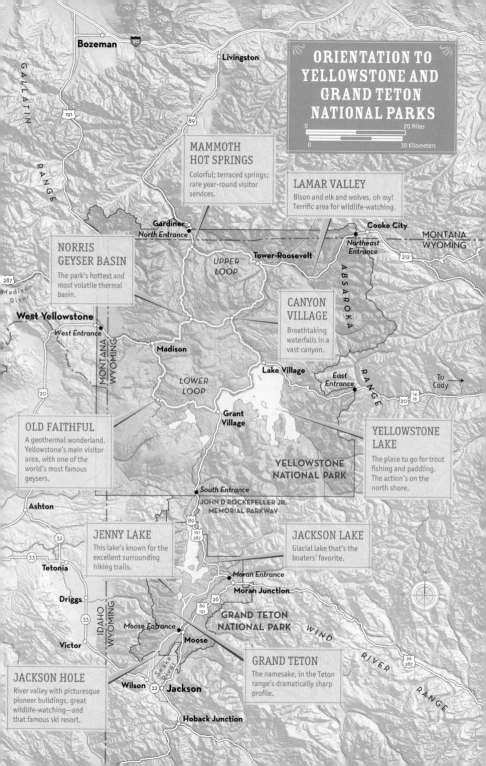

ORIENTATION TO YELLOWSTONE AND GRAND TETON NATIONAL PARKS

0 _____ 20 Miles
0 _____ 30 Kilometers

Bozeman

Livingston

GALLATIN RANGE

MAMMOTH HOT SPRINGS
Colorful; terraced springs; rare year-round visitor services.

LAMAR VALLEY
Bison and elk and wolves, oh my! Terrific area for wildlife-watching.

Gardiner
North Entrance

Cooke City

Northeast Entrance

MONTANA
WYOMING

NORRIS GEYSER BASIN
The park's hottest and most volatile thermal basin.

UPPER LOOP

Tower-Roosevelt

ABSAROKA

Madison River

West Yellowstone

West Entrance

MONTANA
WYOMING

Madison

CANYON VILLAGE
Breathtaking waterfalls in a vast canyon.

LOWER LOOP

Lake Village

East Entrance

RANGE

To Cody

OLD FAITHFUL
A geothermal wonderland. Yellowstone's main visitor area, with one of the world's most famous geysers.

Grant Village

YELLOWSTONE NATIONAL PARK

YELLOWSTONE LAKE
The place to go for trout fishing and paddling. The action's on the north shore.

Ashton

South Entrance

JOHN D ROCKEFELLER JR. MEMORIAL PARKWAY

JENNY LAKE
This lake's known for the excellent surrounding hiking trails.

JACKSON LAKE
Glacial lake that's the boaters' favorite.

Tetonia

Driggs

IDAHO
WYOMING

Moran Entrance

Moran Junction

Victor

Moose Entrance

Moose

GRAND TETON NATIONAL PARK

WIND RIVER RANGE

N

JACKSON HOLE
River valley with picturesque pioneer buildings, great wildlife-watching—and that famous ski resort.

Wilson

Jackson

GRAND TETON
The namesake, in the Teton range's dramatically sharp profile.

Hoback Junction

S T

EXPERIENCES

Trust us, you can't see it all in one trip. At least not without spending months, if not years, in the Greater Yellowstone area and risking a serious grandeur overdose. Not only is there so much to see, there's an incredible amount to do. To help you hone in on the most memorable options, we put together a list of favorite sights and adventures that we feel should shape your itinerary. These are the parks' can't-miss experiences, the places we take our own families and friends when they come out to visit. Let the following pages be a springboard as you head out to rack up some best experiences of your own.

—Brian Kevin, *author*
—Jeff Vanuga, *photographer*

BEST
Waterfall

Lower Falls, Yellowstone; *see p. 170*

"One of the ultimate
(and rare) panoramic
views is from
Artist Point on a
summer morning, when
the falls catch the light.
At sunset, head to
the magnificent,
dizzying **Brink** of the
Lower Falls overlook."

—*Jeff Vanuga*

You might spot a rainbow over the Lower Falls. ▸ ▸

BEST
Backpacking

Paintbrush Divide Trail, Grand Teton;
see p. 213

"Picking the 'best' trail
for backpacking is like
picking the 'best'
breakfast food (they're
all great!), but the
Paintbrush Divide stands
out for **amazing
alpine scenery.**
It's an aerobic hike—
and you might cross
snowfields . . .

Teton peaks seen from the Paintbrush Divide trail. ▶▶

even in late summer—but there are few places in the park where the Tetons seem to envelop you like they do at the 10,500-foot divide. Count wildflower species on your way up and stop to lounge around the glassy lakes straddling the pass. You won't be alone up here, but it's still classic Teton backcountry."

—*Brian Kevin*

The Paintbrush Divide Trail passes String Lake. ▶▶

INSIDER'S PICK

Black Canyon of the Yellowstone

"Spend at least three nights hiking the Black Canyon, a great area to spot wild-life. I met my first eyeball-to-eyeball grizzly here and I'll never forget it."
—*Brian Kevin; see p. 154*

BEST
Thermal Basin

Upper Geyser Basin, Yellowstone;
see p. 71

see p. 71

"I've been here so many
times it's almost ridiculous,
but there's always
something new to see.
Mornings are the
best time to come—
it's showtime!
As the sun lifts, the fog
rises and the geothermal
features emerge, steaming
and bubbling.

Old Faithful Geyser in the Upper Geyser Basin. ▶▶

In spring and fall, this atmospheric microclimate is even more dramatic. Beyond Old Faithful look for spectacular, long-lasting eruptions at the Great Fountain Geyser. If time is short, visit Clepsydra Geyser, which is constantly going off. In winter (my favorite visiting season), you'll see amazing frost formations. Remember to watch where you step."

—*Jeff Vanuga*

Morning Glory Pool in
◀◀ the Upper Geyser Basin.

◯ INSIDER'S PICK
Monument Geyser Basin

"An occasional steam puff is all the activity you'll see at Monument but the backcountry basin's tall, dormant cones are striking—like a silica sculpture garden." —*Brian Kevin;* see p. 116

BEST
Wildlife Watching

Lamar Valley, Yellowstone; *see p. 158*

"Hordes of habitual **wolf-watchers** can't be wrong— Lamar Valley is a broad, grassy mecca for herd animals and the predators and scavengers that follow them. Pull over around dawn or dusk to spot wolves skirting the bison and elk herds. **Bears and coyotes** often lope nearby, too, waiting to move in on a kill. Places like this are why you keep binoculars in the glove box."

—*Brian Kevin*

Lamar Valley is one of the best places to see wolves. ▶▶

BEST
Lodging

Old Faithful Inn, Yellowstone; *see p. 267*
Jenny Lake Lodge, Grand Teton; *see p. 275*

"I could walk into the
Old Faithful Inn every
morning and still go
slack-jawed at the sight
of the lobby, architect
Robert Reamer's seven-
story **tribute** to
wood, air, and shadow.
Absolutely unique."

—*Brian Kevin*

The main lobby of the Old Faithful Inn. ▶▶

"If you find yourself on the porch of the Jenny Lake Lodge one night, maybe admiring the peaks of the Cathedral Group following a five-course dinner, take a minute to breathe in and savor all that woodsy opulence. The all-inclusive lodge is one of the ritziest accommodations in any national park. No wonder you have to reserve at least a year in advance."

—Brian Kevin

A sitting room in Jenny Lake Lodge.

INSIDER'S PICK

Yellowstone Expeditions' winter yurt camp

"After a full day on skis, nothing relaxes you like falling into a down sleeping bag in your own cozy wilderness 'yurtlet.' Though an hour in the sauna yurt helps too." —Brian Kevin; see p. 191

BEST
Scenic Route

Teton Park Road, Grand Teton; *see p. 204*

"I imagine that every 30 seconds or so, a driver somewhere on Teton Park Road says, **'Wow.'** It only takes a couple of miles to see why. Out the window to the west, the Tetons leap up from the horizon so abruptly, they're like a **pop-up display,** and you can really see the glaciers and dikes that give the range its **personality.** Killer photo-ops at each of the roadside pullouts."

—*Brian Kevin*

Teton Park Road is the drive closest to the Teton range. ▶▶

BEST
Day Hikes

Mystic Falls, Yellowstone; see p. 84
Hidden Falls, Grand Teton; see p. 213

"**A waterfall** at the end of a trail is like a big piece of cake at the end of a meal, and these two are among the parks' most alluring. Both hikes are flat and short, good for kids and beginning hikers. Plus you can extend them if you have extra time and energy—the climb to the Inspiration Point overlook above **Hidden Falls** is well worth the effort and much less crowded."

—*Brian Kevin*

A short ride on a Jenny Lake shuttle takes hikers to Inspiration Point. ▶ ▶

Best Panoramic Views

Mt. Washburn, Yellowstone; *see p. 173*

"Climbing Mt. Washburn is a great way to get a nearly 360 degree view of Yellowstone. From the summit, you'll see a mosaic of trees and meadows, with the Teton peaks in the distance. Expansive views like this are rare in Yellowstone. In June, look for bighorn sheep and their lambs; in fall, you'll hear bugling elk."

—*Jeff Vanuga*

Best Campground

Slough Creek, Yellowstone; *see p. 281*

"It's worth rolling into Slough Creek first thing in the morning to beat the fishermen to the campsites along the whispering creek. This campground may be the most tranquil place you can pitch a tent in Yellowstone and still be within a few steps of your car."

—*Brian Kevin*

Best History Lesson

Historic Yellow Bus Tours, Yellowstone; *see p. 99*

"Tour guides in these historic cabs are founts of Yellowstone knowledge. They're also all amateur comedians—laugh at their jokes and they'll tell you anything you want to know. Itineraries aren't always fixed, so just ask if there's something you want to see."

—*Brian Kevin*

Best Fishing

Madison River, Yellowstone; *see p. 117*

"Don't be enticed by the glut of fishermen casting lines around Madison Junction—the river runs through the wildlife-rich Madison Valley for 14 miles, and every serious Yellowstone angler has his or her own favorite stretch. Get friendly with the guides in the West Yellowstone fly shops if you want a couple of pointers on where and what they're biting."   —*Brian Kevin*

Best Places to Eat in the Parks

Lake Hotel Dining Room, Yellowstone; *see p. 99*
Dornan's Chuckwagon, Grand Teton; *see p. 228*

"I like to go to the Lake Dining Room after I've been backpacking, when I'm sick of trail mix and I'm ready for a little silver-spoon treatment—the service is superb. Dornan's isn't the only place in Greater Yellowstone to do the kid-pleasing chuckwagon thing, but nobody does it as authentically as Jackson Hole's original open-air dude diner."
—*Brian Kevin*

Best Lodging in Town

A Teton Treehouse, Jackson Area; *see p. 278*

"I'm not usually a B&B sort of guy, but this inn among the pines has more heart than your usual doily-and-teacup nostalgia shack. I love how the building wraps around and through the trees so you can't glimpse the whole place at once. Owners Denny and Sally know the Tetons and Jackson Hole inside out, so quiz them over homemade breakfast."

—*Brian Kevin*

Greater Yellowstone's History

The aurora borealis, or northern lights, glow
in the sky over Yellowstone National Park.

YELLOWSTONE FIRSTS

FIRST PEOPLES:
Roughly 8,000
B.C.E.

**FIRST MENTION ON
A MAP:** 1797

**ESTABLISHED AS
FIRST NATIONAL
PARK:** March 1,
1872

⟶ YELLOWSTONE'S FIRST INHABITANTS

Eleven thousand years ago, retreating ice sheets from the waning Pinedale glaciation were leading a game of ecological follow-the-leader across the Yellowstone Plateau. In the glaciers' wake came vegetation, followed by birds and small mammals. Then larger game arrived on the scene, and bands of hungry humans weren't far behind. Archaeological evidence indicates that people were occupying greater Yellowstone roughly 10,000 years ago, once they found enough animals and plants there to sustain them.

Yellowstone's first peoples were nomadic hunter-gatherers, criss-crossing the landscape to take advantage of seasonal resources and favorable climates. Blood found on stone points and other tools suggests they had broad tastes in megafauna, hunting everything from bison to elk to big cats, while dispersed pieces of Yellowstone obsidian reveal their extensive migration and trade patterns.

Throughout the last millennia, several tribes, including the Blackfeet, the Crows, and Shoshone, used the Yellowstone area as a travel corridor or hunting grounds. One Shoshone band—the Tukudika, or Sheepeater—was the only group to call the Yellowstone high country home. A peaceable group of bighorn sheep hunters, the Sheepeaters were forcibly removed by the federal government to the

Wind River Reservation in Wyoming in the 1870s. Remnants of their wickiups, or temporary shelters, still stand throughout the park. (Look for groups of aspen poles arranged in a rough pyramid.) Despite ethnocentric pioneer claims that native people feared the park's thermal features, many tribes' oral traditions reveal a spiritual reverence for the geysers and hot springs.

⊙→ THE MOUNTAIN MEN

A Missouri River tributary named "Rivière des Roches Jaunes" got its first ink on the map in 1797, labeled in the language of the French trappers then making inroads into the west. The "yellow stones" in question were probably the sandstone bluffs along the river's lower reaches in what are now eastern Montana and North Dakota—not, as often assumed, the colorful cliffs of the Grand Canyon of the Yellowstone.

Meriwether Lewis (left) and William Clark (right), painted from life by Charles Wilson Peale.

The expedition led by Captain Meriwether Lewis and First Lieutenant William Clark, called the Corps of Discovery, also glimpsed part of Yellowstone's wonders. Clark followed the northern half of the Yellowstone River in 1806 on the Corps of Discovery's return trip. His party came within 50 miles of Mammoth Hot Springs, and though he had heard rumors from the Shoshone of a volcanic area to the south, he pressed on to rendezvous with Lewis at the Missouri River.

One member of the Corps, a rugged Kentucky woodsman named John Colter, stayed behind in Yellowstone country. He wanted to make a go of it trapping beavers—a growth industry at the time, as the fashion scene back east demanded a steady supply of pelts. In the winter of 1807–1808, Colter became the first person of European descent to make a recorded journey through Yellowstone, the Grand Tetons, and Jackson Hole. His old friend Clark published a map of Colter's route in 1814, the first to make mention of Yellowstone Lake and the "hot spring brimstone" of the thermal basins. One hot spring Colter visited near present-day Cody acquired the nickname "Colter's Hell," a label misapplied to Yellowstone off and on ever since.

Trappers told seemingly wild tales of petrified forests and Dante-esque landscapes where steam and boiling water exploded from the earth.

Colter is popularly known as the first of the mountain men, the hardscrabble society of trappers and traders who roamed beaver-rich basins in the northern Rockies throughout the first half of the nineteenth century. As they trapped on behalf of established fur companies, the routes and exploits of the mountain men helped to fill in the maps and fire up the imaginations of settlers in the western territories. Trappers told seemingly wild tales of petrified forests and Dante-esque landscapes where steam and boiling water exploded from the earth. Around today's Yellowstone, infamous trappers and storytellers like Jedidiah Smith, Jim Bridger, and William Sublette have had their names applied to everything from mountain ranges to restaurant desserts.

⟶ FURTHER EXPLORATION AND THE BIRTH OF THE NATIONAL PARK

In the mid-nineteenth century, territorial skirmishes and the U.S. Civil War deflected interest from official exploration of Yellowstone, but the 1850s did see an influx of pickax-toting prospectors. Flush with optimism from the recent California gold rush, mining parties picked up where the mountain men left off after the decline of the Eastern fur market. They added new reports to the sensational descriptions that had newspapers comparing Yellowstone to California's newly famous

Yosemite region. The miners' gilded dreams didn't materialize, but their accounts inspired a few formal expeditions, notably the three-man Folsom-Cook-Peterson expedition in 1869. An eastern magazine published the Folsom party's detailed accounts of Mammoth Hot Springs, the Grand Canyon of the Yellowstone, and the Lower Geyser Basin, conferring some "establishment cred" that miners' and trappers' tales lacked.

Two expeditions in particular brought Yellowstone into the public eye. One was led in 1870 by Henry Washburn, Surveyor General of the newly created Montana Territory. With 19 men and a military escort, the Washburn party took measurements of peaks and canyons, spotted and named Old Faithful, and brought back the first sketches of Yellowstone's natural wonders. In 1871 the director of the U.S. Geological Survey, Dr. Ferdinand Hayden, led 34 men on a scientific survey of the region; his group included landscape painter Thomas Moran and photographer William Jackson. The artists' efforts, com-

Dr. Ferdinand Hayden (above) led one of the earliest scientific expeditions to Yellowstone, traveling with a pack train (right).

bined with the detailed topographic work of Hayden's team, put to rest any doubt about the truth of earlier Yellowstone claims. The expedition produced the most detailed maps to date, and Hayden returned with a team a year later for a similar survey of the Grand Tetons and Jackson Hole.

The origin myth of Yellowstone National Park involves the members of the Washburn party camped along the Madison River on

THE FLIGHT OF THE NEZ PERCÉ

Yellowstone's darkest moment came in the late summer of 1877, when the park became the setting for a dramatic chapter in the tragic flight of the Nez Percé. Fleeing a cavalry division sent to force them onto a reservation, a band of 800 Nez Percé, including women and children, fled their traditional homeland in eastern Oregon and tried to make it across the border into Canada.

After several bloody battles and escapes in Idaho and Montana, the remaining refugees crossed into Yellowstone along the Madison River in late August. Almost immediately, they encountered a small tourist party camped in the Lower Geyser Basin. The tribe took them hostage, wounding several, and crossed the plateau to a ford of the Yellowstone River near Mud Volcano. Scout and warrior parties dispersed through the park, encountering other tourists and killing two at Mammoth and Otter Creek. The Nez Percé released the hostages before escaping the park, squeaking past the Army through a slot canyon along the Clark's Fork of the Yellowstone River.

In October, a remaining 380 people were cornered by the Army less than 40 miles from the Canadian border and forced into surrender. It was here, defeated, that the Nez Percé leader Chief Joseph made his famous statement, "From where the sun now sets, I will fight no more forever." Today, the Nez Percé National Historic Trail commemorates the tribe's route across four states. Though the exact route through Yellowstone is unknown, a wayside exhibit tells the story at Nez Percé Creek south of Fountain Flats Drive.

A Nez Percé man photographed in 1907 by Edward S. Curtis.

September 19, 1870, at the foot of what has since been dubbed National Park Mountain. As the story goes, the explorers debated whether and how they might stake claims to the amazing natural features they had witnessed before deciding that the whole region should instead be set aside as a national park.

Historians have since come to doubt the story, but it is true that, upon their return, members of both expeditions began speaking out in favor of government protection of Yellowstone. The Northern Pacific Railroad supported the plan, as it hoped to cash in on the potential tourist economy. The federal government had only recently ceded the Yosemite Valley to the state of California in 1864, on the condition that it be preserved for public use and recreation, so the concept of a national park wasn't too much of a stretch. Convinced by the entreaties of the explorers, the railroad lobby, and the artful images produced by Moran and Jackson, Congress passed the Yellowstone National Park Act on March 1, 1872. The world's first national park was to be "reserved and withdrawn from settlement, occupancy, or sale," held in common "for the benefit and enjoyment of the people."

EARLY ADMINISTRATION AND ARMY YEARS

Yellowstone National Park got off to a rough start. Congress hadn't actually allocated any funds for the park's management and administration, convinced by supporters' arguments that concessionaire fees could fund the fledgling park once the Northern Pacific Railroad arrived with tourists. The unenviable and unpaid task of managing this experiment went to Nathaniel Langford, a vocal proponent of the park concept and a veteran of both the Washburn and second Hayden expeditions. Still working full-time as a bank examiner in the territories, Langford only visited the park three times before he was replaced as superintendent in 1877.

Lacking any actual caretakers, Yellowstone's first ten years were characterized by poaching, squatting, and profiteering. Congress began providing meager funding for a civilian administration in the early 1880s, but lawlessness in Yellowstone continued. It reached a tipping point in 1886 when, after a series of inept superintendents prompted Congress to revoke the funding, the U.S. Army was placed in charge of the park. In what was supposed to be a temporary stopgap, fifty soldiers marched into Yellowstone in August of that year.

Fort Yellowstone Cavalry—the U.S. Soldiers who guard the great National Park.   Copyright 1903 by Underwood & Underwood.

A 1903 photograph shows U.S. Army cavalry parading near a young Fort Yellowstone at Mammoth Hot Springs. Such soldiers helped form the role of the modern park ranger.

The army ended up running Yellowstone for thirty years, until the National Park Service was founded in 1916.

Yellowstone's Army years represented a sea change in park management. Poachers were pursued and punished, vandalism was discouraged, and shady park entrepreneurs had a military body to answer to. The era also saw the construction of the park's Grand Loop Road and many of its soaring hotels. For the soldiers staffing Yellowstone, patrolling the two-million-acre wilderness required fortitude and long hours on the back of a horse. Because the Army initially lacked legal authority to do much more than expel a criminal from the park, punishments for vandals or poachers were creative. In some cases, soldiers would march the apprehended miscreant all the way across the park to the southern boundary, informing the offender he could pick up his confiscated posessions from Army headquarters—80 miles away, at the north entrance.

Being equal parts law enforcement, game warden, and tour guide was an awkward post for some soldiers, and desertion rates were high at first. But as the Army matured into its administrative role, Yellowstone's soldiers helped to establish the template for the modern park ranger. Their ability to adapt to a more civilian-like role helped smooth the transition when the National Park Service took over Yellowstone in 1916.

Early motorists drive past the Shoshone Dam towards Yellowstone.

On following pages: (top left) at Sapphire Pool; (bottom left) looking sharp while descending by rope into the Grand Canyon of the Yellowstone; (top right) wading in the Great Fountain Geyser; (bottom right) the first known boat on Lake Yellowstone, circa 1871.

☉⟩ A MODERN PARK

In 1882 the Northern Pacific railroad finally reached Livingston, Montana, and rail travel became a central element of the Yellowstone experience. By 1908 the gateway towns of Gardiner, West Yellowstone, and Cody all had train depots. The railroad companies, led by the Northern Pacific, poured money into the expanding park hotels and concessions. Visitors arrived by rail by the tens of thousands, and by the 1920s and 30s, by the hundreds of thousands. Typical Yellowstone tourists in the early twentieth century were well-heeled Easterners out to play the dude. Clad in light suits, golf skirts, and linen dusters, they saw the park via stagecoach tours and stayed in lodges, while more adventurous and less affluent tourists bunked in elaborate tent camps.

Cars came to Yellowstone in 1915 and forever changed the national park experience. As Yellowstone grew increasingly auto-centric, the two rings of stagecoach routes known as the Grand Loop Road became entrenched as the central means of seeing the park. The rise of the automobile and an increasingly prosperous nation kept visitation stats climbing, reaching a fever pitch in the years following World War II. Park visitation doubled from prewar numbers, surpassing a million annual visitors in 1948. Marginalized by auto traffic, the rail-

A bear cub "holdup." Lax regulations in the park's postwar era encouraged wildlife to beg for food.

YELLOWSTONE AND GRAND TETON NATIONAL PARKS

roads abandoned Gardiner, West Yellowstone, and Cody one by one. When the modern incarnation of Grand Teton National Park was established in 1950, the two linked parks became the classic American summer vacation. Visitor numbers doubled again by the mid-1960s, and today around three million people visit Yellowstone each year.

With more park visitors came more congestion on the roads, more foot traffic near the park's major attractions, and a larger commercial circus in the towns adjoining the park. The modern environmental ethic evolved—and indeed, is still evolving—in this atmosphere. Harmful wildlife practices, like the tradition allowing bears to feed in public view at park dumps, began to be phased out during the 1950s and '60s. Gradually, NPS moved toward a policy that sought to balance visitor-service demands with the needs of Yellowstone's unique ecology. Visitor education on ecological issues became a bigger priority. The growing strength of the new environmental ethic emerged in the late 1960s, when biologists initiated the first quiet calls for the reintroduction of wolves (*see* the Geology, Flora, and Fauna chapter).

The sweeping fires of 1988 dramatically illuminated the complex ecological relationships at work inside Yellowstone. The previous NPS policy of fire suppression had already been reformed to allow for controlled burns, but Yellowstone was long overdue for a big blaze. During the very dry summer, the accumulated fuel built up during years of misguided fire policy fed more than a dozen large and small forest fires. Despite fire crews' heroic efforts at control, the fires scorched over a third of the park before being extinguished by damp weather in the fall. You can see the fires' fascinating ecological effects today in acres of eerily beautiful "ghost forests," where new plant and animal species have gained a foothold among the maze of blackened poles.

The park's administration and advocates continue to address ecological issues of enormous complexity, everything from fire management to trout management to snowmobile management—all while debating how much "management" any given element of the Yellowstone ecosystem should receive. What characterizes the intricate decision-making processes in Yellowstone now is the tightrope effort to balance the visitor experience and the demands of conservation biology. For instance, when the park adopted a catch-and-release policy for all native game fish in 2001, that move was accompanied by a new emphasis on fish-watching as a guest activity. The search for balance in Yellowstone is perpetual.

THE LONG ROAD TO GRAND TETON

While the campaign to establish Yellowstone National Park succeeded inside of two years, the genesis of Grand Teton National Park was a strung-out affair, jam-packed with power struggles and political intrigue. From its inception, the National Park Service had its eye on Jackson Hole at the Tetons, but skeptical ranchers, hunters, and homesteaders actively resisted the loss of grazing lands and the threat of commercialization. Locals got antsy, however, when the state proposed a dam on scenic Jenny Lake, and their grudging support led the way to the "first" Grand Teton National Park in 1928.

The 1928 park included only the mountains themselves and a handful of lakes in their shadow, leaving out the lion's share of Jackson Hole. Enter billionaire tycoon and philanthropist John D. Rockefeller Jr., whose visits to the valley in the 1920s convinced him of the need for federal protection. With support from the NPS, Rockefeller's Snake River Land Company spent two decades buying up Jackson Hole—

32,000 acres of it—as insurance against ranchers and developers. His repeated attempts to "gift" the land to the NPS were rebuffed by Wyoming's congressional delegation, which feared the loss of tax revenues if the valley became federal land. In 1942, a fed-up Rockefeller threatened to sell his holdings if the government wouldn't take them. This prompted President Franklin Roosevelt to establish Jackson Hole National Monument by executive order—an end-run around Congress.

Reactions from angry locals included a protest run of 500 cattle across the new monument. But dissent quieted down during World War II, and in the postwar boom, the locals heard the cash registers ringing around Yellowstone. In 1950, popular support finally led to the merging of park and monument, creating the Grand Teton National Park we know today.

A Teton panorama, with Jackson Lake in the foreground.

Yellowstone's
Lower Loop

The aptly named Beauty Pool in the Upper Geyser Basin.

An evening wind buffets
Castle Geyser in the Upper
Geyser Basin.

Clepsydra Geyser erupting in the Lower Geyser Basin.

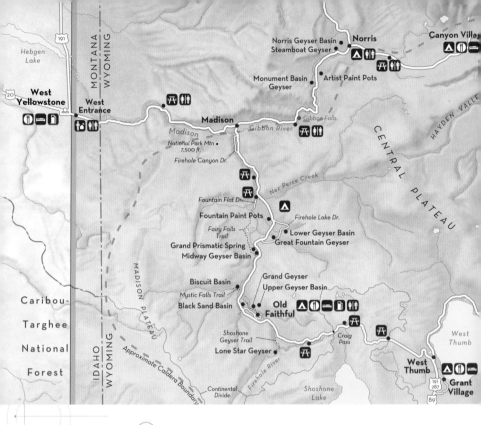

OLD FAITHFUL

AMOUNT OF WATER
IN AN ERUPTION:
3,700 to 8,400
gallons

AVERAGE
INTERVAL: 90
minutes or so

OLD FAITHFUL VILLAGE

*See the Yellowstone National Park: Lower Loop and Around
Old Faithful maps.*

More than any other natural features in the park, the surreal thermal
basins along the Firehole River are responsible for Yellowstone's earliest
and most enduring nickname, "Wonderland." The area's explosive
fountains and kaleidoscopic springs make wide-eyed Alices out of even
the savviest geyser-gazers. Veteran hydrogeologists and field-tripping
third graders all break into dumbstruck grins when Old Faithful sends
its 150-foot column of water hissing into the sky.

It's always been this way. After the genteel explorers of Henry
Washburn's expedition first saw Giantess Geyser erupt in 1870,
Washburn wrote, "Our usually staid and sober companions threw up
their hats and shouted with ecstasy at the sight."

The Upper Geyser Basin around the Old Faithful village contains
a full one-fifth of the world's geysers, with more than 200 spouters

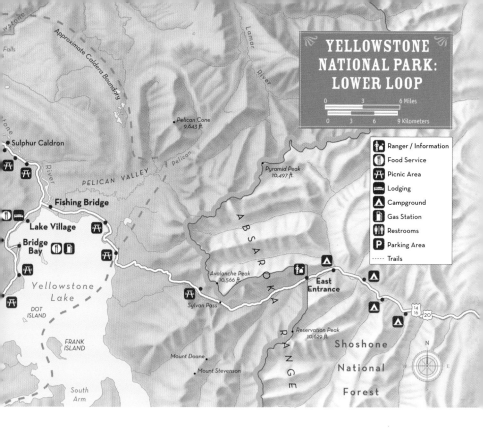

PELICAN VALLEY

Fishing Bridge

Lake Village

Bridge Bay

Yellowstone Lake

DOT ISLAND

FRANK ISLAND

South Arm

Sulphur Caldron

Pelican Cone
9,643 ft.

Pyramid Peak
10,497 ft.

ABSAROKA

Avalanche Peak
10,566 ft.

Sylvan Pass

East Entrance

Reservation Peak
10,629 ft.

RANGE

Mount Doane

Mount Stevenson

Shoshone

National

Forest

Approximate Caldera Boundary

Falls

Lamar River

Pelican

14
16
20

YELLOWSTONE NATIONAL PARK: LOWER LOOP

0   3   6 Miles
0   3   6   9 Kilometers

Ranger / Information
Food Service
Picnic Area
Lodging
Campground
Gas Station
Restrooms
Parking Area
----- Trails

crammed into less than two square miles. This corner of the park is a global geyser clearinghouse, because it has a rare combination of an underground heat source, sufficient water, and the right plumbing system. (*See* Spotlight on Geothermal Features *and* the Geology, Flora, and Fauna chapter.) The conditions to create a geyser field like this one occur in only a handful of locations worldwide.

Exactly what Yellowstone's native groups made of these thermal wonders has been the subject of curiosity and misunderstanding since the arrival of the first fur trappers. Only recently have researchers and anthropologists begun to learn some of the stories passed on through various oral traditions. One of the most evocative tales comes from the Kiowas of Oklahoma, whose ancestral lands bordered the upper Yellowstone River. The tribe tells of a Kiowan hero led by the creator spirit, Doh Ki, across a bleak volcanic landscape in search of a homeland for his people. The tribe followed the hero through the land of steam and boiling

★ *Inspiring Geyser* ★

Morning Glory Pool inspired the popular children's book *Hedgie Blasts Off!*, in which a hedgehog goes to another planet to unclog a geyser clogged by space tourists' debris.

water, eventually reaching the cave known today as Dragon's Mouth. Doh Ki tested the hero by promising to give him the surrounding lands if he leapt into the bubbling spring. When the hero met the challenge, he was plucked from the scalding water to find a lush, bountiful land around him—today's Yellowstone National Park.

The early tourist trade at Old Faithful erupted with the same suddenness and force as its spouting geysers. No sooner had Yellowstone received its first federal appropriation in 1878 than a rough-and-tumble road was pushed through to the Upper Geyser Basin. Guided tours reached the basins shortly thereafter, followed by temporary camps; by 1882 the Northern Pacific Railroad was surveying the region for a possible rail line.

By 1885, Old Faithful had its first hotel, a flimsy pine structure that even Yellowstone's assistant superintendent decried as "a shack and a disgrace to the park." But such hasty development gradually tapered off, and except for a few missteps over the years (like a naval searchlight placed atop the hotel to light the geysers at night), hospitality facilities at Old Faithful were designed with an eye to the long term. The Old Faithful Inn and the Basin Store are among the oldest park structures still in use.

Observation Point is a good place to watch Old Faithful erupt from a distance.

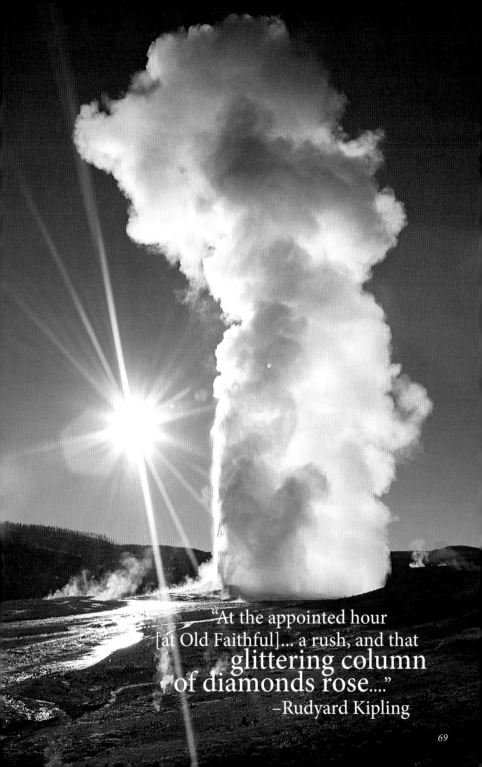

"At the appointed hour
[at Old Faithful]... a rush, and that
glittering column
of diamonds rose..."
–Rudyard Kipling

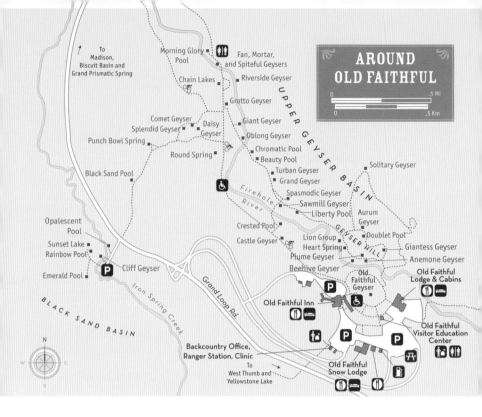

The village today is the main tourist zone, with several places to eat and stay, two gas stations, two general stores, and a state-of-the-art visitor center slated to open in 2010. Robert Reamer's 1903 Old Faithful Inn is the crown jewel of national park lodging, looming above the geyser basin like a feudal castle. In the summer, some 25,000 visitors pass through the Old Faithful area each day, and lumbering snowcoaches from West Yellowstone and Mammoth make the rounds in winter. It's important to stay on boardwalks and trails, both for safety's sake and to protect the fragile landscape. But don't be too turned off by the crowds—the basins and backcountry in the Old Faithful region have plenty of grandeur to go around.

OLD FAITHFUL
VISITOR
EDUCATION
CENTER

TEL:
307/545–2750

THE GEYSER BASINS

Not all of Yellowstone's geysers can be as faithful as you-know-who; prediction is an inexact science. Geysers' complex underground plumbing is affected by earthquakes and other subterranean hijinks that geologists are only beginning to understand. It's a dynamic system, where some spouters spring to life and others fall dormant with little or no warning. Upcoming predicted eruption times are sometimes posted in the basins, and the **Old Faithful Visitor Education Center** (307/545–2750) posts times for the powerhouses Old Faithful, Riverside, Daisy, Grand, Castle, and Great Fountain. The center also offers a schedule of guided geyser walks, from ten-minute strolls to half-day hikes.

Plan a half-day at the very least to walk the boardwalks of the **Upper Basin.** (It really takes two or three days at Old Faithful to see eruptions from each of the major geysers. At any given time, though, you're almost guaranteed to see some sort of geyser action.) ★**OLD FAITHFUL** is easy to pick out—it's surrounded by a huge boardwalk and a few hundred people. Across the Firehole River is **Geyser Hill,** a treasure trove of geysers large and small. Among the standouts is **Beehive Geyser,** a squat cone with enormous jets of up to 190 feet. Beehive settles in and out of periods of regularity, but you can usually count on at least one show a day during the summer. There's an indicator vent in front of the cone—when it starts steaming a full geyser blast is not far behind. **Giantess Geyser** is another prominent resident of the hill, and though she usually averages just a few magnificent eruptions per year, the roar of steam during these can be heard up to a mile away.

Grand Geyser erupts in a series of beautiful and violent spurts, capturing rainbows in its spray.

From Geyser Hill the boardwalk follows the Firehole River to the northwest, then loops back along a paved trail, with a few spurs branching off along the way. There's a viewing platform set up at **Grand Geyser,** and inevitably there's a small crowd waiting to see 200-foot bursts from the world's largest predictable geyser. Roughly every eight to nine hours, Grand erupts in a series of beautiful and violent spurts, capturing rainbows in a spray that dampens the giddy spectators. Farther up the boardwalk, the massive cone of **Giant Geyser** looks like a surfacing whale in a sea of sinter. (The sinter, or silica deposit, has a coarse texture like tree bark.) It's the world's second-largest geyser when it erupts, with a spray that can reach 250 feet and last for an hour. Since the Hebgen Lake Earthquake in 1959, Giant has "on years" and "off years." There were only six eruptions between 1963 and 1987, but more than 50 in 2007 alone.

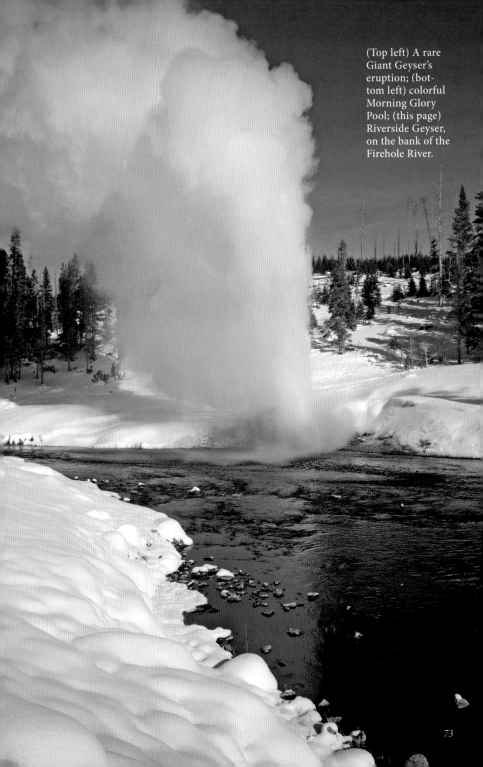

(Top left) A rare Giant Geyser's eruption; (bottom left) colorful Morning Glory Pool; (this page) Riverside Geyser, on the bank of the Firehole River.

Excelsior Geyser discharges more than 4,000 gallons of boiling water into the Firehole River every minute. When active, it was the largest geyser in the world.

Farther along the paved trail, **Riverside Geyser** sends a 70-foot arc of water out over the Firehole River every six to seven hours, making it one of the basin's most predictable geysers, as well as one of its most beautiful. **Morning Glory Pool** is worth the walk to the pavement's end, as its concentric circles of brilliant orange and aqua signal the bacterial life that thrives in the superheated water. In the past, visitors have inconsiderately tossed coins and other items into the spring, affecting its temperature, color, and water circulation. Heading back toward the village along the paved trail, you'll pass **Castle Geyser** near a bridge over the river. Castle's whopping 12-foot cone is evidence of at least 5,000 years of continual activity, and the name bestowed by the Washburn party perfectly captures its imperial stature. It erupts two or three times a day with intervals from four to fifteen hours.

You can drive to **Black Sand Basin,** a half-mile north of the Old Faithful exit, though the walking trail from the Upper Basin winds its way there as well. This is a quick stop, with thermal features more subtle than in the neighboring basins. The most alluring feature at Black Sand is not a geyser at all but **Emerald Pool,** a broad hot spring that gets its dreamy translucent greenness from cyanobacteria living on the crater walls.

Biscuit Basin (Grand Loop Rd., 2 mi north of Old Faithful) demonstrates the paradox of naming sights in such a volatile landscape. The basin was named for a cluster of funny biscuit-shaped geyserite formations that flanked the crystal-blue **Sapphire Pool.** But the major 1959 earthquake tweaked Sapphire's internal plumbing, and the once placid pool exploded with 125-foot eruptions that demolished the namesake biscuits. Today Sapphire Pool gurgles and boils but is a dormant spring once more.

Midway Geyser Basin (Grand Loop Rd., 10 mi south of Madison Junction) is the more pedestrian name for what park visitor Rudyard Kipling called "Hell's Half-Acre" in 1889. ★**GRAND PRISMATIC SPRING** is the main draw; it's the world's third-largest hot spring at more than 370 feet across. The pool's vivid red and orange colors drizzle down its runoff channels, but from the boardwalk you can only glimpse a portion of these psychedelic tentacles. For the full picture, follow a faint, unofficial "social" trail up the 250-foot **Midway Bluff,** across the highway and a quarter-mile south. There are also good photo ops along the Fairy Falls Trail (*see below*). Lest you start thinking of geysers as just cute little underground fountains, witness the massive crater around **Excelsior Geyser,** evidence of its cataclysmic eruptions before going dormant in the 1880s.

Thank the little guys:
          heat-loving microorganisms
(bacteria and algae) tint the

Grand Prismatic Spring

with a rainbow of colors.

It's like dropping a boulder into a kiddie pool. Great Fountain Geyser's eruptions can be almost as wide as they are tall.

OLD FAITHFUL

Before Old Faithful became the world's first celebrity geyser, it was just another spouter in the Upper Geyser Basin, waiting for its big break. But this particular geyser is separated from other major features by a good 400 yards, so its unshared underground plumbing system allows for relative predictability. Members of the Washburn party noticed that consistency in 1870, and though earthquakes in 1959 and 1983 affected Old Faithful's intervals, the name the Washburn party thought up is still accurate.

Old Faithful erupts every 60 to 90 minutes, depending on the previous eruption's length. The closest viewpoint is the surrounding semicircular boardwalk. Another popular place to watch is the Inn balcony just above the carriage porch, where you can relax in a deck chair facing the geyser. There's also a seldom-mentioned second-floor vantage point that fits a few people, where the old Inn joins the east wing. For a great photo, head up Geyser Hill and stand near the Sponge and Pump geysers; you'll get the landmark Inn in the foreground. A slightly taxing half-mile walk to Observation Point puts Old Faithful's 100- to 180-foot plume against a backdrop of wooded hills.

A crowd gathers for the most popular show in Yellowtone National Park.

So many rushed visitors opt to bypass the one-way, three-mile **Firehole Lake Drive** (Grand Loop Rd., 9 mi south of Madison Junction) that you can sometimes take in its thermal wonders in relative solitude. The big dog in this southern unit of the **Lower Geyser Basin** is **Great Fountain Geyser,** which erupts in a series of angled, 100-foot bursts every nine to eleven hours (predicted at the Old Faithful Visitor Center). Even between eruptions, pools of water on the fountain's vast, tiered sinter platform are a gorgeous sight. It was here in 1869 that the Cook–Folsom party became the first "respectable" (non-Native American, non-mountain man) group to witness a Yellowstone geyser eruption. It's also worth pulling over to examine the peaceful simmering pool of **Firehole Lake and White Dome Geyser,** an erratic splasher with a 20-foot cone that looks like a pile of lumpy oatmeal.

The wide, watery explosions of **Fountain Geyser** every half-hour or so are the main attraction at **Fountain Paint Pots** (Grand Loop Rd., 8 mi south of Madison Junction), along with near-perpetual 20- to 40-foot bursts from **Clepsydra Geyser.** The namesake mud pots are the most interesting feature, though, blurping and gurgling as muddy bubbles burst, flinging flecks of confetti-like clay in all directions. Iron in the mud oxidizes at differing rates, giving some mud clumps a pinker hue than others.

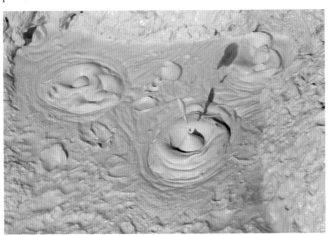

Mud pots pop and gurgle in Pocket Basin.

Fountain Flat Drive (Grand Loop Rd., 6 mi south of Madison Junction) marks the northern edge of the Lower Basin. This old service road remains open to cars for about a mile, almost as far as **Ojo Caliente Hot Spring.** The deep-blue "hot eye" gives off great clouds of

JUNIOR RANGERS

Three bucks and a rigorous course (wink) of scientific study is all that stands between your 5- to 12-year-old and the elite status (and patch!) of a Junior Ranger. Grab a program guide from any park visitor center, then get to work completing worksheet activities, hiking a trail, and participating in a ranger-guided education program at one of the villages. (See the park newspaper for ranger-program schedules.) If one patch isn't enough, a similar Young Scientist program at the Old Faithful and Canyon visitor centers issues kids a magnifying glass and infrared thermometer for important field research.

steam and discharges about a hundred gallons of water per minute into the Firehole River. Geysers and springs cluster along the riverbanks. Though a number of fishermen's trails skirt the banks, it's best to follow someone who knows where they're going through this dangerous area. Very worth your time is a four-hour, ranger-led hike through the mud-pot mecca of **Pocket Basin,** visible to the east of the paved drive but trail-less and treacherous. The hike leaves from Old Faithful twice a week in summer; check at the visitor center for details.

NEARBY SIGHTS

The park service broke ground on a new **Old Faithful Visitor Education Center** (307/545–2750) in the summer of 2008, with plans to open a 26,000-square-foot, two-story facility by the fall of 2010. This will have a research library, auditorium, and a mess of interactive exhibits on Yellowstone's hydrothermal marvels. In the meantime, the temporary stand-in center is pretty humble, just a glorified trailer with an assistance desk and a decent-sized bookstore. Rangers are helpful as ever, though, and you can still find the posted times for geyser eruptions.

An army lieutenant with the Washburn party in 1870 observed of the 150-foot **Kepler Cascades** (Grand Loop Rd., 2.5 mi south of Old Faithful), "[t]hese pretty little falls, if located on an eastern stream, would be celebrated in history and song; here amid objects so grand… they were passed without a halt." Halt at the roadside pull-out for a good photo opportunity, or pick your way down to a wooden bridge at the foot of the falls to feel a bit of its cool spray.

BEST HIKING TRAILS

The **Fairy Falls Trail** through Midway Geyser Basin leads you to four striking sights in an easy, very flat 6.5-mile round-trip. Start a mile south of the Midway Basin lot, at the south end of the gravel Fountain Freight Road. Right away you cross a historic steel bridge, then it's a

An NPS worker ready to roll in a tour bus.

YELLOWSTONE
433 · PARK

mile along the abandoned road grade to the junction with the trail. As you pass Grand Prismatic Spring to the east, get a photo-perfect view by scrambling up the hill to your left. Leaving the gravel, the trail goes through forests hit hard by the 1988 fires. You'll hear splashing from the 197-foot falls before you see it, a delicate-looking ribbon that tumbles into a perfect swimming pool. Less than a mile ahead is the last wonder, Imperial Geyser, a broad blue pool that's been active throughout the 2000s.

It's just a one-mile, flat hike to the sublime namesake of the ★MYSTIC FALLS TRAIL, where young pines frame a tiered, 70-foot cascade as steam rises from the Little Firehole River. The whole scene, boxed in by sloping rock walls, has the feel of a secluded nook—which it can be during spring and fall, though this is a popular hike during peak season, especially with families. Shake some of the crowd by completing the whole three-mile loop, past the falls and up some moderately taxing switchbacks to an overlook at almost 8,000 feet. The loop ends back at the trailhead on the far side of Biscuit Basin, and views of steam rising from the Upper Basin are worth the effort.

An overnight hike to the **Shoshone Geyser Basin** is an opportunity to experience a boardwalk-free, backcountry thermal area without having to go off-trail. This mostly flat, nine-mile hike begins along the paved route to **Lone Star Geyser,** at the trailhead just south of the Kepler Cascades. A well-defined trail follows the upper Firehole River through unburned lodgepole, rising only mildly across the Continental Divide, then descending along quiet Shoshone Creek to the basin. The trail winds through some of the basin's remote, hundred-plus thermal features—if you choose to explore off-trail, use caution and common sense. You'll hear the waves of Shoshone Lake from inside your tent at nearby shoreline campsites.

OTHER ACTIVITIES

Cycling is a top activity around Old Faithful; you'll have more options here then anywhere else in the park. The **Bear Den** (307/545–4825) gift and gear shop at the Old Faithful Snow Lodge rents mountain bikes throughout the summer.

From Old Faithful village the paved trail through the Upper Geyser Basin meets an abandoned service road near Daisy Geyser that runs 1.5 miles to Biscuit Basin. North of the village, the Fountain Freight Road picks up where Fountain Flat Drive ends. This four-mile stretch of gravel, which once had the Monopoly-esque handle of National Park Drive, now leads bikers through elk-frequented meadows in the Lower and Middle Geyser basins.

Another good bet is the 2.5-mile ride to Lone Star Geyser. Yellowstone's Army administration built the stagecoach road to this geyser in the early 1890s, and the flat, paved, two-mile route wasn't closed to auto traffic until 1971. The geyser's isolation, consistent three-hour eruption intervals, and tank-like 11-foot cone make it one of the most enjoyable geysers to visit.

WHERE TO EAT

Old Faithful Inn Dining Room. A massive, two-story, volcanic stone fireplace strikingly anchors this historic dining room. Original timber ceiling beams, hickory chairs, and copper chandeliers all recall the days when meals were served with silver and china, though there's no need to dress for dinner today. Buffets are at the heart of every meal, with a few sandwiches added to the lunch menu and a handful of additional entrées at night. The classic Old Faithful dinner is farm-raised bison, carved onto your plate at the buffet table. After dinner, have a cocktail at the leather-topped tables in the adjacent and equally historic Bear Pit Lounge. *Old Faithful Inn; 307/344–7311 or 866/439–7375.* **$$$–$$$$**
Obsidian Dining Room. A long row of east-facing windows lets in natural light during breakfast and lunch here, while candelabras shaped like pine trees glow in the evening. Rotating comfort-food

specials might include goulash or lamb stew. Vegetarians can opt for a fried green tomato entrée or eggplant with orzo—improvements on the typical pasta-or-veggie-burger choices. The Firehole Lounge, separated from the dining room by a two-sided fireplace, serves creative appetizers and might be the only room in the park going for a sleek, contemporary look instead of the usual woodsy decor. *Old Faithful Snow Lodge; 307/344–7311 or 866/439–7375.* **$–$$$**

Geyser Grill. Funky decor gives the Geyser Grill more character than Yellowstone's other fast-food options. The room's dividing wall is shaped like a mountain, and stuffed-animal voyageurs peer over the edge of a canoe hung from the ceiling. Collect your basic burgers and breakfast sandwiches on a cafeteria tray. The first-come-first-served seating gets jam-packed during the summer, but you can always pull up some concrete on the shaded porch. *Old Faithful Snow Lodge; 307/344–7311 or 866/439–7375.* **$–$$**

Old Faithful Lodge Cafeteria and Bake Shop. The cafeteria itself is a drab, fluorescent-lit cluster of lunch and dinner stations serving pizzas, pastas, and the like, but the dining space is a grand hall of pine and stone dating back to the 1920s. Settle into a woven-cane chair by the massive windows and drink in a superb view of Old Faithful. Breakfast isn't served in the cafeteria, but there's an espresso cart, and the cinnamon rolls at the tiny bakery can get you through a morning of geyser-gazing. *Old Faithful, east end of village; 307/344–7311 or 866/439–7375.* **$–$$**

Old Faithful Basin Store. This historic building was park entrepreneur Charles Hamilton's first commercial venture way back in 1897, and the ornate, knotty-pine facade still reads "Hamilton Store." You'll find the best budget breakfast in the village in the small cafeteria. Thick blueberry pancakes and buttery French toast are a steal at around six dollars. Burgers, salads, and sandwiches make up the lunch menu, and if you eat on the porch, they come with an excellent view of Geyser Hill. *Old Faithful, northwest of Inn; 307/545–7282.* **$**

LAKE VILLAGE

See the Around Yellowstone Lake map.

For a while there, during the first half of the nineteenth century, it seemed like **Yellowstone Lake** was the one thing everybody could agree on. Early accounts from Yellowstone's mountain men, miners, and mapmakers disagreed about the directions of rivers and the sources of

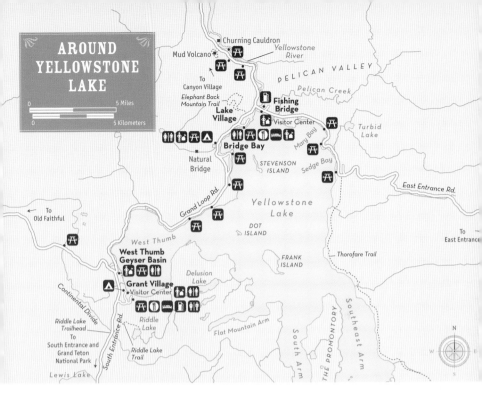

the implausible-sounding hot springs. But they all agreed on the lake. Trapper Jim Bridger exaggerated its size as 60 miles across, and early government cartographers wrongly drew it in the shape of an oval, but the wide expanse of Yellowstone Lake has always been a landmark to explorers.

On first glance, Yellowstone Lake seems pale and placid and permanent, a steadfast body in a landscape celebrated for unpredictability. It's an act, though. Not only is the 136-square-mile lake prone to rough water and sudden storms, but on the scale of geologic time it's perhaps the park's most dynamic feature. It once extended all the way into Hayden Valley, some ten miles north, and it may have originally discharged to the south, joining the Snake River and, eventually, the Pacific Ocean. After the last Ice Age, tectonic action and the deepening of the Yellowstone Canyon shifted its momentum northward, into the Yellowstone River, draining into the Atlantic via the Missouri and the Mississippi. Since the mid-1990s, scientists have monitored rising underwater domes in the lake's northern reaches, features that are slightly "tipping" the lake, enlarging beaches on the north shore and

"No other lake in North America
of equal area lies so high as
the Yellowstone,
or gives birth to so noble a river."
– John Muir

The bison herds in Hayden Valley are most impressive from mid-July to August, when burly males try to out-macho one another by locking horns and kicking up dust.

Hayden Valley's Crater Hills Geyser is a rare sight, as it's off-trail in a grizzly-bear habitat.

A BAD DAD TALE

suggesting that the lake may someday tilt enough to "switch back" and drain to the south.

These days, the lake's north shore has all the action, with the historic **Lake Village,** the bustling marina at Bridge Bay, and the gaggles of sightseers at Fishing Bridge and its visitor center. Summer visitors to Lake Yellowstone should expect heavy traffic and plan to stop frequently at the many lake overlooks between West Thumb and Bridge Bay. By contrast, the land south of the lake is some of the park's most remote country, where a long backpacking trip brings you as far from a paved road as you can get in the continental United States.

NEARBY SIGHTS

The thermal grotto at **Mud Volcano** (Canyon–Lake Rd., 6 mi north of Fishing Bridge) is dwarfed by those surrounding Old Faithful, but its springs and fumaroles have as much character as any of the park's thermal features. The sharp smell of sulfur hits you hard as you approach the basin's namesake. Mud Geyser was once a powerful 30-foot cone, but sometime before 1872 a particularly vicious eruption blew the cone away, leaving only a muddy, gurgling crater.

Along the same boardwalk is **Dragon's Mouth Spring,** a cave that audibly roars as seething waters crash against its cavern walls. Farther up the hill, the mesmerizing **Churning Cauldron** stews at an average temperature of 164 degrees Fahrenheit, sloshing and steaming as if a monster might emerge at any minute. **Sour Lake** spreads out behind the basin's boardwalks. The bluish pool looks innocent enough, but a submerged forest of dead trees attests to a pH level somewhere in the neighborhood of battery acid. Set aside at least an hour to see and smell everything in this area.

Just north of Mud Volcano, the landscape opens up into a treeless plain once drowned beneath the swollen waters of glacial Yellowstone Lake. **Hayden Valley** is one of the park's finest spots for wildlife-watching in any season; in summer it's a hangout for grizzlies, elk, wolves, and especially bison. The herds are most impressive from mid-July to August, when bison from throughout the park congregate in the valley for the rut, or breeding season, burly males trying to out-macho one another by locking horns and kicking up dust. The Yellowstone River meanders through the grassland; here you might spot pelicans and cranes, as well as a few families of river otters. Dusk and dawn are the best times for viewing, though the roadside pull-offs stay full throughout the day. Don't expect to pass through Hayden Valley in a hurry—if the bison aren't causing traffic jams then the people watching them are.

At **Fishing Bridge** (East Entrance Rd., .5 mi south of Grand Loop Junction) the Yellowstone River leaves the lake to wind north toward Canyon. The current log-and-concrete bridge, with pedestrian walkways, went up in the late 1930s. Critical cutthroat spawning grounds made this a popular place to wet a line for decades, and ironically, it's also why the area was closed to fishing in 1973. Grizzlies love trout almost as much as fishermen, though, and you may spot a bruin or two from the bridge in early summer. The **Fishing Bridge Visitor Center** (307/242–2450) is an impressive gabled hut made of hewn logs and boulders the size of easy chairs. Inside is a circus of taxidermy, one of the few places you're likely to see a legally mounted bald eagle or trumpeter swan.

You can find some great souvenir bargains on the second floor of the **Fishing Bridge General Store** (East Entrance Rd. at Fishing Bridge; 307/242–7200), a "sales loft" of discounted grizzly-bear sweatshirts, Old Faithful Inn collectible plates, and other Yellowstone keepsakes. The only lodging at Fishing Bridge is an RV park, but services include a gas station and general store, and the area stays packed all summer with folks arriving and departing via the East Entrance.

FISHING BRIDGE VISITOR CENTER

TEL:
307/242-7200

Best Hiking Trails

The flat 1.5-mile hike to ★NATURAL BRIDGE is probably the best short hike in the park in terms of the sweat-to-scenery ratio. From the trailhead at Bridge Bay marina, a short jaunt through a pine forest reveals a 50-foot arch reminiscent of southwestern sandstone formations. A few gentle switchbacks lead to the top of the bluff, but hikers should stay off the fragile formation. A hare-brained plan for a stagecoach route over the arch failed in the late 1870s, but cars accessed Natural Bridge until 1991 on what's now a separate bike trail. Because of frequent bear activity, the area is off-limits in the spring.

Hiking near the
Mud Volcano in
winter.

Pack a picnic before setting out for the forested hilltop known as **Elephant Back.** The lake overlook on top is a perfect site for an outdoor family lunch, and you'll probably be hungry after gaining 800 feet in two miles. The lollipop loop is four miles start to finish, beginning on the north side of the road a half-mile east of Lake Village Junction. You'll see spruce and fir trees in the woods along the way, boldly defying the tyranny of the dominant lodgepole pine. If you can get to the summit by sunrise, you'll see the lake spread out like a dark blanket before the orange-tinted Absarokas.

The Yellowstone River cuts a lush, green passageway as it squiggles through the jagged Absaroka Mountains in the southeast corner of the park. Trappers nicknamed this easily navigable route the Thorofare. A trip along the 33-mile **Thorofare Trail** requires at least a weeklong commitment. It's a true classic among backcountry adventures. The route follows the lake's eastern edge and runs past a chain of 10,000-foot peaks to the park's southern boundary—and from there it's a grueling hike out via the South Boundary Trail or the Bridger-Teton National Forest. But the West's most unspoiled country is its own reward, promising unsurpassed solitude, abundant wildlife sightings, and a dozen campsites with jaw-dropping panoramic views.

OTHER ACTIVITIES

Bridge Bay has come a long way since explorer David Folsom described the idyllic inlet in 1869 as "a beautiful little lake…fashioned by the practised hand of nature, that man had not desecrated." It's still wooded and scenic, but tourism has the upper hand now. The natural bay was dredged in the early 1960s to construct the **Bridge Bay Marina** (Grand Loop Rd., 2 mi south of Lake Village; 307/344–7311 or 866/439–7375). The area stays packed with recreational boaters, fisherman, and strolling families from the adjacent campground. Among the boats docked at Bridge Bay is the *Lake Queen*, a 44-foot tour boat that makes hour-long interpretive trips around Stevenson Island. These cruises leave six or seven times a day between June and mid-August.

Eighteen-foot outboards are available for hourly rental at Bridge Bay, and you can get a humble rowboat for a couple hours or an overnight trip. Guided sightseeing trips run from $150 for two hours on a small boat to more than a grand for a full-day on a 34-foot monster.

Chartered **fishing trips** (866/439–7375) include guide, tackle, and fishcleaning. The gorgeous native cutthroat trout is catch-and-release only, but if you're trolling deeper water, you're likely to pull in one of the many invasive lake trout. Illegally introduced sometime in the

1980s, the larger fish devour the cutthroats, and their rapid colonization of the lake spells ecological disaster, since cutthroats are an important food source for raptors and grizzlies. The only rules governing lake trout are that you must kill and report any you catch.

Paddling along the shore of Lake Yellowstone can be one of the wildest and most scenic experiences in the park. Outfitters offering day trips and guided, multiday tours include Jackson's **Snake River Kayak & Canoe** (365 N. Cache St.; 307/733–9999), whose ebullient guides are as talented with a camp stove as with a paddle. If you want to explore without a guide, you'll need your own boat or a rental from outside the park.

Many paddlers set out along the undeveloped eastern shore from the **Sedge Bay Boat Launch** (East Entrance Rd., 8 mi southeast of Fishing Bridge), heading toward one of four backcountry campsites within a leisurely three-hour paddle. The lake's south and southeastern arms are thick with waterfowl and see very little motorized traffic—in fact, the lower reaches of each are closed to motors altogether. The most expedient route to these stunning and silent shores is via the **lake shuttle,** which drops off and/or picks up you and your boat at an agreed-upon location. Call the Bridge Bay Marina direct (307/242–3876) to set up a shuttle.

Yellowstone Lake stays icy cold throughout the year, and the threat of hypothermia is a serious one. Sudden winds can make for abruptly choppy conditions, particularly on the eastern shore. Kayaks offer a bit more stability than most canoes, but both craft should stick to the shore—open-water crossings can be very dangerous.

On the outside looking in at the Lake Hotel sunroom and lounge.

WHERE TO EAT

★LAKE HOTEL DINING ROOM. Sunlight spills from huge windows into this vast, open room. Lake's dining room has a deserved reputation for the best food in the park, particularly at dinner. You might start out with a shared plate of rich lobster ravioli before tucking into Montana-raised tenderloin with rosemary-cabernet sauce. The sandwiches at lunch are a cut above, with choices like Black Forest ham and artisan cheeses. (The breakfast buffet, though, doesn't stand out.) *Lake Village; 307/344-7311 or 866/439-7375.* **$$$-$$$$**

Lake Lodge Cafeteria. This warm, wood-beamed space hasn't changed much since it was built in 1920. The place gets packed at mealtimes, particularly breakfast and dinner, when families from the neighboring cabins pour in for eggs and bacon or a plate of pasta or fish. In the main lodge room there's a popular bar next to a hulking stone fireplace. The wide porch overlooking the lake, complete with rocking chairs, is easily the best spot in Yellowstone to unwind with a cocktail. *Lake Village; 307/344-7311 or 866/439-7375.* **$-$$$**

Fishing Bridge General Store. With pancakes, French toast, and omelets, the cheap breakfast menu at Fishing Bridge beats out the other general stores' prepackaged morning offerings. The snack bar doesn't have much seating, but you can make lunch and dinner alfresco at the picnic area across the road. *East Entrance Rd., at Fishing Bridge; 307/242-7200.* **$**

Lake Hotel Deli. The deli is really more of a snack stand, offering a small menu of inexpensive sandwiches and sweets from late morning through late evening. Cheese sandwiches and PB&Js make this perhaps the only place in the park to feed the kids for under three dollars. Take your meal around the corner to the elegant sunroom to feel like you're having a more polished meal than you paid for. *Lake Village; 307/344-7311 or 866/439-7375.* **$**

OLD YELLER BUSES

The yolk-yellow antique touring buses spotted along Yellowstone's roads date back to the 1930s. Whole fleets were retired in the 1960s, but in 2007 eight of the classic vehicles were restored and returned to service. The buses' nicknames reflect how they spent the second half of the twentieth century. "Monty," for instance, was owned by a Vermont collector, while "Hollywood" starred (bizarrely) in *Big Trouble in Little China*. For info on getting on board, *see* the Practical Information chapter.

Lake General Store. The cheap breakfast and lunch items won't win any culinary accolades, but you can get in and out of this location relatively quickly after an egg-and-cheese biscuit or premade panini. The counter is tiny and the seating sparse, but the cedar-framed, octagonal store dates back to 1922, and it's worth a visit just to check out the kooky architecture. *Lake Village; 307/242-7563.* **$**

GRANT VILLAGE AND WEST THUMB

See the Yellowstone National Park: Lower Loop map.

Southwest Yellowstone remains something of an undiscovered country to most visitors. Though the area lacks an easily accessible "name" attraction like Old Faithful or the Grand Canyon, the sheer number of natural wonders—from waterfalls to hot springs to massive backcountry lakes—rivals any other region of the park. It wasn't until almost 40 years after Yellowstone became a national park that the southwest corner finally got its own ranger station, and the wet and wooded landscape remains remote and roadless still today.

The flooded volcanic basin known as the West Thumb of Yellowstone Lake is named for the lake's vague resemblance to an upside-down hand. **Grant Village** is on its south shore. In some respects the black sheep of the Yellowstone hospitality family, the village was established in the 1960s by the NPS's controversial Mission 66 program (*see* the Where to Stay chapter), which sought to modernize and "green" Yellowstone's visitor facilities, but sometimes did ecological damage of its own. Grant Village, for instance, was the result of relocating facilities from the environmentally fragile West Thumb and Fishing Bridge areas, but the village was constructed in prime grizzly habitat. Because of this clash, the campground is closed during the trout-spawning season in May and early June when bears come to feed.

CASCADE CORNER

Hidden within the forested acres of Yellowstone's wild southwestern corner are more than a hundred known waterfalls, earning the area its nickname. Known more formally as the Bechler region, after its most prominent river, Cascade Corner is hemmed in by two plateaus, and the abundant creeks and streams pouring off the plateaus' sloped edges create chains of stunning ivory falls. This country is remote yet extremely popular with backpackers; it's a great place to spot moose. Because backcountry hot springs empty into a lot of the streams, secret soaking spots are almost as tempting to hikers as the waterfalls.

The dated facilities at Grant lack the rustic-historical vibe of much of the rest of the park, but it has an off-the-beaten-path feel that attracts many dedicated explorers. It's also the best launching pad for day trips into the Tetons. Paddlers line up at the boat launch to explore the bay's bluff-lined coast, and on the wind you can smell the blue-green tartness of the lake.

WEST THUMB GEYSER BASIN

The West Thumb is actually a caldera within a caldera. A volcanic explosion here 150,000 years ago caused the land to collapse in on itself, and the hole filled with water to become the West Thumb of Yellowstone Lake. The thermal basin here has always been known more for its beauty than its action, and in the high water of spring and early summer many of the features are actually submerged, giving them a cool, sunken-treasure look. West Thumb is also a rare opportunity to see all four varieties of thermal features within just a few steps of one another.

The **West Thumb Visitor Information Station** (no phone) is a squat 1925 log cabin, worth a peek in the winter when it's a cozy warming hut. The building is a bookstore in the summer, and it's usually crowded. You'll find a posted schedule of guided ranger programs; call the nearby Grant Visitor Center (307/242–2650) for more information.

Check out an example of mud pots at the **Thumb Paint Pots,** which have grown increasingly soupy in the past 40 years. During low-water periods they can still spit their semi-solid clay far enough to form funky, gloppy mud cones. On the other side of the geyser basin is the dark emerald trench of **Abyss Pool.** At 53 feet, it's the deepest hot spring known in Yellowstone. Though unpredictable, **Surging Spring** is the most entertaining West Thumb feature to watch when it's active. The light blue pool looks innocent, but every five or ten minutes it gurgles up and floods the lake with some 2,400 gallons of water. Meanwhile, the fumaroles on the west end of the boardwalk hiss angrily as they release ribbons of steam.

On the lake side of the boardwalk, **Lakeshore Geyser** and **Fishing Cone** are the most visually arresting formations at West Thumb. Their two cones peek up from the water like one-eyed, geyserite sea monsters. When the water level is low, Lakeshore can very rarely erupt to 25 feet. Fishing Cone is dormant and acts as a hot spring. Yellowstone's early visitors bragged of catching fish while standing on it, then turning around and boiling their catch in the spring. Damage

Visitors brave the February cold to explore the West Thumb Geyser Basin.

The vent of Blue Funnel Spring in West Thumb Geyser Basin seems to shift as you walk past the pool—an optical illusion at work.

to the cone suggests this was indeed attempted, and needless to say fishing is no longer permitted from Fishing Cone.

Technically, this is the only frontcountry geyser basin where you don't have to stay on the boardwalk—but that's just because you have the option of paddling. **O.A.R.S.** (800/346–6277) leads trips twice daily in summer from Grant Village. The half-day ★WEST THUMB KAYAK TRIPS take you past the main basin and farther up the shore to a cluster of springs called the Lake Shore Group, only accessible by water. Gliding past the cones and springs at eye level offers a completely different perspective and a truly unique view of thermal features. Only paddlers see the swirls and eddies that mark hydrothermal vents hidden in the lake bottom. (It's a great photo opportunity, too.)

Nearby Sights

Architecturally, **the Grant Village Visitor Center** (307/242–2650) is the least interesting of the park's interpretive facilities. It does house an excellent display on the 1988 forest fires, though, reminding visitors it's a miracle that Grant Village still exists. The Shoshone fire in 1988 completely surrounded Grant, forcing two evacuations and coming within 100 feet of several buildings. In summer, rangers host a nightly kids' program on the center's back porch, discussing wildlife and geography with some hands-on props.

It's a two-mile round-trip stroll to the **Lake Overlook** across the road from the West Thumb Geyser Basin. The route is so gentle it can't even be called a hike. A scant gain of 200 feet (easier if you take the loop clockwise) leads through a patchwork of unburned spruce and fir stands alternating with new lodgepole growth—evidence of the 1988 fires. The overlook itself offers views across the choppy waters of the West Thumb, with the Absaroka Mountains looming distantly to the southeast.

Mama porcupine nuzzling Junior and the migratory mountain bluebird, Yellowstone's harbinger of spring.

Ten miles south of Grant, the 30-foot **Lewis Falls** makes for a good photo op; the Lewis River pours in a fat cascade off the lip of the erosion-resistant caldera and cuts into the softer rock below. From here, the Lewis heads south toward the Snake River, carving out the 350-foot deep Lewis Canyon on the east side of the South Entrance Road. The pullout for the falls' overlook is small and gets very crowded with folks on foot, so drive with caution.

Best Hiking Trails

The flat, easy **Riddle Lake Trail** is all the more special for being closed half the year. From spring until July 15 the area is off-limits for bear

PEOPLE IN THE PARKS:
"DIGGER" JERRY GEORGE, WRITER

"DIGGER" JERRY GEORGE is a trained high-altitude ecologist. Since 2004 he's been a *San Francisco Chronicle* columnist, filing dispatches from wild places across the country—particularly Yellowstone, where he spent three years as a de facto "embedded reporter."

Brian Kevin: So you lived *inside* the park?

Jerry George: I essentially was the baggage—it was my wife who had the reason to live in the park, teaching elementary school [for children of employees] at Mammoth.

BK: What other work goes on in the park behind the scenes, that visitors usually don't see?

JG: I'm blown away by what Xanterra [the park concessionaire] accomplishes. In seven weeks they go from having no hotels open to all hotels open. They go from no employees to nearly 5,000 trained employees. How does Xanterra accomplish that?

BK: Your columns are often about the unique natural details you observe. What can visitors do in order to start noticing the types of things an ecologist notices?

JG: When I was a photojournalist in Vietnam, I was viewing and defining the world in terms of what made a "good shot." And I failed to see anything outside of that "good shot." You have to learn *not* to look for specific things—that's like looking through a camera. If you let yourself fall into that trap, you don't notice the things that ultimately may be the real message.

BK: Given all your park experience, what makes Yellowstone stand out?

JG: All life in Yellowstone has been extinguished five times in the last two million years—maybe six. And look at what it is today. Yellowstone does more to renew our faith in the ability of the planet to persevere than any other place.

It's humbling. And yet, the humbling that Yellowstone does is not a debilitating humbling. It's actually an empowering humbling. It leaves you feeling comfortable that it's not all on your shoulders. In fact, it doesn't give a damn about your shoulders at all. And that's a healthy thing for people to realize.

management, but the rest of the year the 2.5-mile route leads through a quiet, partially burned forest and over the Continental Divide. Because there's almost zero elevation gain, it's likely the easiest crossing of the divide you'll ever attempt. (It's a big favorite for families.) The lake seemed like a "riddle" to early explorers because it was thought to have straddled the divide, draining in two directions. Alas, it's just north, and it drains directly into Yellowstone Lake via the snarkily named Solution Creek. Watch for moose in the marshes, as well as a variety of waterfowl. Find the trailhead two miles south of Grant on the east side of the South Entrance Road.

The **Heart Lake Trail** allows for trips of various lengths, but a hike to the shoreline campsites about eight miles in is one of the best short backpacking trips in the park. Along the way, hikers cross wildflower meadows, smell sulfur from fumaroles and hot springs along Witch Creek, and maybe glimpse an active geyser. Five idyllic campsites line a vast, blue stretch of Heart Lake, in the shadow of 10,308-foot Mount Sheridan. A strenuous three-mile climb leads to a lookout shelter and sweeping views of the Yellowstone Plateau and the Tetons. On cold mornings, steam pours from the Heart Lake Geyser Basin like a science project gone awry, making for a spooky hike out. Head out from the trailhead five miles south of Grant on the east side of the South Entrance Road.

The second-highest falls in the park, ★UNION FALLS is a magnificent, thunderous cascade where Mountain Ash Creek pours in a dramatic pyramid over a 265-foot rock wall. You'll feel the spray even from the overlook, some hundred yards away. The falls is at the end of a moderately strenuous eight-mile hike through the unburned forests of the Cascade Corner district. It's a tough day hike, but two backcountry sites along bubbling Mountain Ash Creek allow for overnight trips. You can also take a dip in a naturally warmed swimming hole a half-mile below the namesake falls. Find the trailhead just outside the park's southern boundary on Grassy Lake Road, 10 miles west of Flagg Ranch.

OTHER ACTIVITIES

The interconnected Shoshone and Lewis lakes dominate the southwest quadrant of Yellowstone. You can set out to hike their shorelines from trailheads along the South Entrance Road or the Grand Loop Road near Old Faithful, but you can only get out on the water via the **Lewis Lake boat launch,** 8.5 miles south of Grant.

While paddlers will have a field day on the combined lakes, motorized boaters are restricted to Lewis Lake. Lined with silent, sandy beaches, Lewis also has hot springs off the northwest shore, offering ideal soaking spots where the warm waters drizzle into the lake. There are no tours or boat rentals offered, though, so these waters are limited to those who bring in their own craft.

Stretching across 8,000 acres, Shoshone Lake is the largest backcountry lake in the continental United States, an inland sea at 7,800 feet that keeps its ice until mid-June. Shoshone is a paddler's dream, surrounded by gorgeous campsites and teeming with wildlife, from abundant brown trout below the surface to impossibly large, white pelicans skimming it. The only access is via Lewis Lake downstream, by paddling up the shaded Lewis Channel, which may require wading and pulling your boat. Because of the effort involved, a trip to Shoshone is at least an overnight affair.

Like Yellowstone Lake, both Shoshone and Lewis lakes are prone to high winds and aggressive waves in the afternoon. Neither gets particularly warm, and turning over a canoe or kayak can spell disaster. Avoid open-water crossings.

Not two miles inside the park's south entrance, a small pullout allows a glimpse at 30-foot **Moose Falls.** The frothy little falls is pretty to look at but more renowned among park staff as a top-notch swimming hole. Thermals upstream keep temperatures warmish, and the pool below the falls is large and deep enough for a gaggle of swimmers. The truly bold can take a 20-foot plunge from a notch just to the left of the falls.

WHERE TO EAT

★ Insider Tip ★

The staff of the Grant Village Dining Room migrates into the postage-stamp bar as they come off shift, so it's a great place to pick up insider tips.

Grant Village Dining Room. The focal point of this long, open room is a wall of windows facing the lake—unfortunately, the pine trees outside obscure the view. The daily three squares are familiar fare, but a standout bison meatloaf puts a Western spin on a comfort-food fave. Vegetarians should expect slim pickings. (Reservations are required for dinner.) *Grant Village; 307/344–7311 or 866/439–7375.* **$$–$$$**

Lake House Restaurant. You can do only breakfast and dinner at the Lake House, but pizzas and pastas are handled ably, and the breakfast buffet is nearly identical to the one at Grant's table-service counterpart and at a slightly lower price. You can also grab a local Snake River Pale Ale and stroll on the shoreline deck overlooking the retired marina. Lake views are unobstructed here, and three of the four walls are all windows. *Grant Village; 307/344–7311 or 866/439–7375.* **$–$$**

Grant Village Grill. The lines are often long, but they move quickly in this small fast-food stand inside the general store. Almost everything is in sandwich form: breakfast croissants, cheeseburgers, chicken sandwiches. This is the fastest place in the village to get a milk shake or root-beer float, and it has the most seating of any of the snack shops. *Grant Village General Store; 307/242–7266.* **$**

⌖ MADISON AND NORRIS

See the Madison and Norris map.

After the earth heaved during Yellowstone's last major volcanic event, it collapsed in on itself, leaving a crater so large it's difficult even to recognize it without an aerial view. But the rim of the Yellowstone caldera is clearly visible between Madison and Norris junctions, a gray ridge of jagged cliffs that parallels the road west of Gibbon Falls. This proximity of the caldera's rim characterizes the rough-hewn landscapes surrounding Norris and Madison, and the scenery gets a boost from the nearby Gallatin Range and the tumbling Gibbon and Madison rivers.

Norris borrows its name from Yellowstone's second superintendent, Philetus Norris, a transplanted Easterner known to patrol the park dressed head-to-toe in buckskins. He built the first road to the

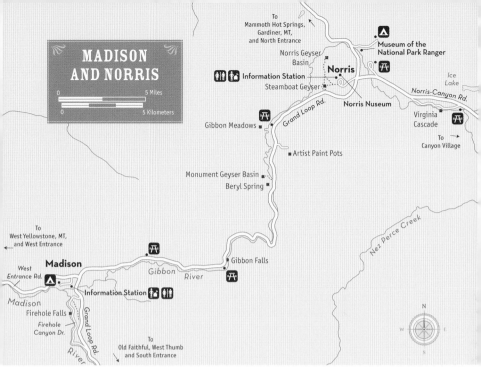

Norris geyser basins in 1878, and the area has been an important crossroads since.

Today Norris and Madison both host hordes of campers in the summer, though neither offers the same breadth of services as the larger villages. You won't find gas stations, groceries, or dining facilities, but there are more picnic sites surrounding Norris and Madison than just about anywhere else in the park. Otherwise, each junction has a few basic amenities, like bathrooms and pay phones.

Norris Geyser Basin

The hottest and most volatile thermal basin in the park sits at the intersection of three fault lines. Those cracks in the earth allow energy from Yellowstone's underground magma pool to heat the ground water more easily. They also make for a network of geysers and hot springs that's constantly changing in response to geologic disturbances. On the surface, the colorful mats of heat-loving microorganisms swell and fade with changes in water temperature and acidity. More than any other basin in the park, Norris is in constant flux.

Two miles of trails and boardwalks weave through Norris's Porcelain Basin and Back Basin. Staying on the boardwalks in thermal areas is always important, but even more so in Norris, where water temperatures over 200 degrees Fahrenheit and extremely low pH levels pose an even greater threat. Located between the two basins, the **Norris Museum** (307/344-2812) has a detailed geology exhibit and a Yellowstone Association bookstore. Schedule a couple of hours to thoroughly explore the one-of-a-kind Norris basin.

Starting out in the Porcelain Basin behind the museum, the first feature you'll encounter is **Black Growler Steam Vent.** A cluster of hissing holes in a barren hillside, Black Growler emits a thick tower of steam that occasionally switches from one hole to another—nobody knows why. The three sporadically active geysers named **Constant, Whirligig,** and **Pinwheel** often support some of the basin's most colorful thermal mats. Stripes of jade, rust, and traffic-cone orange stretch out along the basin floor.

On the museum's south side, the sprawling Back Basin is a buffet of thermals spread out over a modestly forested plain. **Emerald Spring** is a boiling pool tinted an exquisite green by sulfur deposits. Farther along the boardwalk, colorful **Cistern Springs** is constantly overflowing. Its waters are heavy with silica, and formations below the water line look like barnacle-crusted remains of ancient shipwrecks. In the basin's southeast corner, **Echinus Geyser** is the world's largest acidic geyser, with a pH similar to that of vinegar. Pebbles around this geyser have a prickly-looking coat of sinter. Echinus's once-frequent eruptions have been rare and erratic since the late 1990s, a case study in the perplexing changes that sometimes sweep through Norris.

MADISON
INFORMATION
STATION
- - - - - - - - - - - - - - - -
TEL:
307/344-2821
- - - - - - - - - - - - - - - -

The real thermal rock star at Norris is **Steamboat Geyser.** Seeing the world's tallest active geyser erupt is a little bit like seeing a total eclipse, only rarer and utterly unpredictable. Steamboat can go years without a major eruption, but when it does, as it did in 2005, water sprays 300 feet into the air, and the steam plume might double that. The steam phase following an eruption lasts hours, and the roar can be heard for miles. Steamboat sometimes has mini-eruptions of 10 to 40 feet, and its gnarled cone is worth examining even in dormancy.

Nearby Sights

Formerly a soldier station for Army troops, the **Museum of the National Park Ranger** (Mammoth–Norris Rd., 1 mi north of Norris Junction, no phone) traces the evolution of the park's guardians. Display cases hold an array of early park uniforms and tools, and a short film examines the rangers' complex roles as both tour guides and law enforcement. The museum is staffed by retired rangers and NPS employees, and when business is slow they're happy to relax on the back porch and chat about park secrets and lore. Take advantage.

A three-mile scenic cut-off hugs a wooded cliff to lead past the 60-foot **Virginia Cascade** (Norris–Canyon Rd., 1.5 mi east of Norris Junction). It's tough to catch a glimpse as you drive by—there's no established pullout and the trees obscure the view—but the white veil of the falls stands out against the piney backdrop. Try to imagine the first Norris–Canyon Road, which arrived at the foot of the falls before climbing out of the canyon along the steep cliffs; it must've been sheer terror for stagecoach drivers.

The meadows along the Madison River are wildlife hot spots, and at the picnic area next to the **Madison Amphitheater** (Grand Loop Rd., .2 mi south of Madison Junction, no phone) you're almost certain to share your lunch hour with a cluster of grazing elk, especially in fall. The amphitheater faces National Park Mountain, and legend says the Washburn party camped in this meadow when they first proposed national park status in 1870. Check inside the adjacent historic **Madison Information Station** (307/344–2821) for schedules of astronomy programs, concerts, and other summer events at the amphitheater.

Unquestionably the giggliest attraction in all of Yellowstone, the **Artist Paint Pots** (Norris–Madison Rd., 4 mi south of Norris Junction) are a group of heated, chowder-like mud pools that bubble and spurt in continuous, extra-noisy, flatulent outbursts. Explorer Nathaniel Langford compared the texture of the bubbling glop to "the consistency of thick paint" and complained of "a villainous smell" with each burst bubble. The best pots at Artist are at the top of the hilly, mile-long boardwalk loop. These fling mud as high as 15 feet.

It's a quick stop to admire the beautiful **Gibbon Falls** (Norris–Madison Rd., 5 mi east of Madison Junction), which you can't miss from the road. Here the Gibbon River slides in smooth diagonal ribbons 84 feet down a shelf created by the caldera rim. The river and falls were named for an Army colonel who explored the park in 1872, so don't believe the tale—often repeated by mischievous park employees and guides—that the Asian lesser ape was once native to Yellowstone.

Describing **Beryl Spring** (Norris–Madison Rd., 5 mi east of Norris Junction) in the 1921 edition of his *Haynes Guide*, Yellowstone's first guidebook writer, F. Jay Haynes, cautioned, "The violent boiling of its surface, together with the hiss of escaping steam, causes some nervous apprehension to the feelings of the traveler." Though the spring is

Fly-fishing on the Firehole River.

named for the gemstone with which it shares its aquamarine color, Beryl hovers around 200 degrees Fahrenheit, and it's recognized as much for its massive steam discharge as for its color. There's a small viewing boardwalk next to the road.

Best Hiking Trail

It's a wickedly steep climb to ★MONUMENT GEYSER BASIN, but it's nonetheless Yellowstone's easiest backcountry thermal basin to reach. If you have any itch to explore a thermal area without the distractions of crowds, cars, and boardwalks, the trail to Monument Basin is a must-hike.

The trail begins on the west side of the road a half-mile north of Beryl Spring, and gently follows the Gibbon River for the first three-quarters of a mile. Look for trumpeter swans in fall and winter, plus steam from mid-river thermals. The trail doubles back suddenly to ascend the adjacent hill, a gain of more than 600 feet in less than a mile, with views of the Gibbon Canyon and wide, grassy Gibbon Meadows. You'll smell the thick sulfur aroma before reaching the basin. In addition to fumaroles and hot springs, long-dormant geysers at Monument have formed beautiful and alien sinter cones, tall gray cylinders that seem to reach up from the ground like deathly fingers. Remember to stick to the trail and keep your distance from the features.

OTHER ACTIVITIES

Not far from Madison Junction you can track down a rare NPS-acknowledged **swimming hole.** The one-way Firehole Canyon Drive leaves the Grand Loop Road a half-mile south of Madison, shadowing the Firehole River as it runs between 700-foot rock walls. The forty-foot Firehole Falls is pretty enough for a photo op, but the real action along the two-mile cutoff is upstream from the falls. Here the avowedly anti-swimming NPS has given in to the popularity of a long-utilized swimming hole and has installed changing stations, parking, and a stairway. The unstaffed swimming area is rocky, but a great place to stop on a warm day. The current is slow, so it's relatively safe for kids.

Along the West Entrance Road, the Madison River is a meadow stream, a 23-mile stretch full of weedy pools hiding fat rainbow and brown trout. It's a terrific place for **fly-fishing** in early summer and fall. (Avoid midsummer, when high temperatures from the Firehole tributary send the fish away.) Dry fly-fishing is especially popular on the Madison, and no fewer than five outfitters in West Yellowstone are permitted to guide trips. With elk crowding the banks and the mountain views, few trout streams are more picturesque.

Bison and elk jams are common near Gibbon Meadow.

Spotlight on
GEOTHERMAL FEATURES

Windows into the Earth: it's a frequently repeated metaphor for the geothermal wonders that make the Yellowstone landscape so exceptional. More than half the world's thermal features are found in Yellowstone National Park, including some 10,000 hot springs, mud pots, and fumaroles, plus 300 or so active geysers. You'd need to search two or three other continents for as many geysers as you can see during a single afternoon around Old Faithful. If these geothermal features are the Earth's windows, then Yellowstone is like its sun porch, a place unlike any other spot on the globe, where you can peek in on the effects of extreme pressure and heat that are usually hidden deep within our planet.

◄◄ Castle Geyser erupts in its steam phase.

HOW DO GEYSERS WORK?

A few main ingredients make geysers possible: abundant water, a heat source, a certain kind of plumbing system, and rock hard enough to withstand some serious pressure. The layout of any one geyser's underground plumbing is a mystery, but we know that below each vent is a system of fissures and chambers, with constrictions here and there that prevent hot water from rising to the surface. As the underground water heats up, these constrictions and the cooler surface water "cap" the whole system, keeping it from boiling over and ratcheting up the underground pressure. When a few steam bubbles eventually fight their way through the constrictions, the result is like uncapping a shaken-up soda bottle, when the released pressure causes the soda to spray.

GEYSER FAQs

Old Faithful's surface water temperature? 204° F before eruption.

Hottest geyser basin? Norris, with water 1,000 feet below ground at 450° F.

Tallest geyser? Steamboat at Norris, more than 350 feet.

Strangest geyser name? "Deleted Teakettle" at Upper Geyser Basin.

Word origin? From "Geysir," Iceland's earliest known geyser.

Monument
Geyser Basin

Norris
Geyser Basin

Lower
Geyser Basin

Upper
Geyser Basin

West Thumb
Geyser Basin

**YELLOWSTONE
NATIONAL PARK**

Beehive Geyser has an indicator vent in front of its cone. When the vent steams, an eruption is on the way.

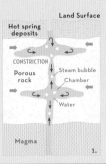

Land Surface

Hot spring deposits

CONSTRICTION

Porous rock

Steam bubble

Chamber

Water

Magma

1.

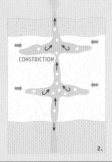

CONSTRICTION

2.

① RECHARGE STAGE

Groundwater accumulates in plumbing and is heated by magma chamber. Some hot water flashes to steam and bubbles try to rise toward surface.

② PRELIMINARY ERUPTION STAGE

Pressure builds as steam bubbles clog at constriction. High pressure raises the boiling point, preventing superheated water from becoming steam.

CONSTRICTION

Pressured steam

3.

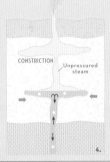

CONSTRICTION

Unpressured steam

4.

③ ERUPTION STAGE

Bubbles squeeze through constriction, displacing surface water and relieving pressure. Boiling point drops. Trapped water flashes to steam, forcing water out of chambers and causing chain reaction.

④ RECOVERY STAGE

Eruption ends when chambers are emptied or temperature falls below boiling. Chambers begin to refill with ground water and process begins again.

A **cone geyser** like Lone Star Geyser has a spout-like formation around its vent, formed by silica particles deposited during eruptions.

A **fountain geyser** like Daisy Geyser erupts from a vent submerged in a hot-spring-like pool. Eruptions tend to be smaller and more sporadic.

BACKCOUNTRY THERMAL AREAS

Not every thermal basin in Yellowstone has a boardwalk and a parking lot. Dozens of geyser and hot spring groups bubble away in the backcountry, miles from the nearest road. Reaching them may be as easy as following a day-hike trail or as tough as backpacking off-trail with a map and compass. Standing alone next to a steaming hot spring, in untouched country, is a truly wild and sublime experience. It can also be very dangerous, as no signs or guard rails warn about unstable ground. Backcountry basin seekers should consult rangers before heading out and always use extreme caution. My favorite remote thermals include the hissing Witch Creek fumaroles near the Heart Lake Trail and the scrappy spouters along the Seven Mile Hole Trail.

Lone Star Geyser is fairly easy to reach, at the end of a former roadway.

No trail reaches the Gibbon Hill Geyser Group, though steam can be seen from the road south of Norris on cool days.

A crust of mineral deposits around the Doublet Pool hot spring.

A thermal pool in the Rabbit Creek Thermal Area.

Essentially, what keeps a hot spring from becoming a geyser is a lack of constriction in its underground plumbing. Like their more explosive cousins, hot springs consist of water that seeps into the earth, only to simmer its way back up through fissures after it's heated by magma. Unlike in constricted geysers, water in a hot spring can circulate by convection. Rising hot water displaces cooling surface water, which then sinks underground to be heated by the magma chamber and eventually rise again. Thus the whole soup keeps itself at a gurgly equilibrium. As it rises, superheated water dissolves some subterranean minerals, depositing them at the surface to form the sculptural terraces that surround many hot springs.

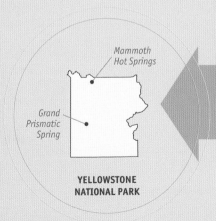

Mammoth Hot Springs

Grand Prismatic Spring

YELLOWSTONE NATIONAL PARK

HOT SPRINGS

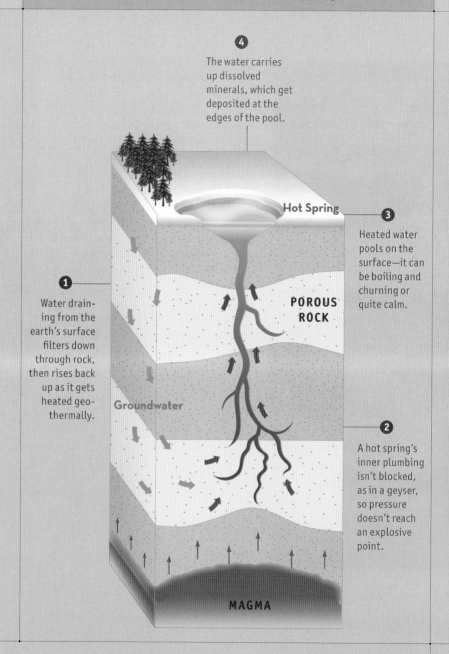

4 The water carries up dissolved minerals, which get deposited at the edges of the pool.

Hot Spring

3 Heated water pools on the surface—it can be boiling and churning or quite calm.

1 Water draining from the earth's surface filters down through rock, then rises back up as it gets heated geothermally.

POROUS ROCK

Groundwater

2 A hot spring's inner plumbing isn't blocked, as in a geyser, so pressure doesn't reach an explosive point.

MAGMA

The vivid colors that characterize hot springs and their terraces can be attributed alternately to minerals like sulfur and iron or to thermophiles. Thermophiles are microorganisms that thrive in extremely high temperatures. Blooming in thick bacterial mats, they convert light to energy, like plants, and their bright photosynthetic pigments help give hot springs their rainbow hues. Scientists suppose only a small percentage of Yellowstone's thermophiles have been identified. Still, these microbes have had a big impact on science. In 1965, a microorganism called *Thermus aquaticus*, or Taq, was discovered in the Lower Geyser Basin. From it, scientists extracted an enzyme that revolutionized molecular biology, ultimately making possible both DNA fingerprinting and the mapping of the human genome. NASA is among those performing research in the park today, studying thermophiles to gain insight on extraterrestrial life.

The Giant: Grand Prismatic Spring, Yellowstone's largest and deepest hot spring.

The Stank Bomb: Sulfur Cauldron, one of Yellowstone's most acidic springs.

The Life of the Party: Punch Bowl Spring.

The Perpetual Spouter: Firehole Spring.

WHAT'S THAT SMELL?

Most people think it smells like rotten eggs, though I've also heard "burnt gunpowder" and "paper mill smokestack." Whatever simile you settle on, there's no question that hot springs and other thermal features stink to high heaven. This sulfur smell occurs when a spring's superheated water dissolves trace amounts of sulfates found in the porous rock below. The sulfates bond with hydrogen in the water to form the stinky chemical hydrogen sulfide, which bubbles up to the surface. In high concentration, hydrogen sulfide can actually kill you, but the small amounts released by thermals can only kill your appetite. It's because hydrogen sulfide is often present in volcanic areas that we associate brimstone (or sulfur) with the underworld.

At the Mammoth Hot Springs terraces, sulfur is dissolved from the mineral gypsum.

Sulfur and other chemicals contribute to springs' acidity, leading to dead vegetation as here at Mammoth.

WHAT ARE MUD POTS?

MUD POT FAQs

Source of "paint pots" nickname? Iron and other metals tinting the mud red and orange.

Where's the biggest cluster of mud pots? Pocket Basin in Lower Geyser Basin.

How big was Mud Volcano before it exploded in 1872? 30 feet tall by 30 feet wide.

Original name of West Thumb Paint Pots? Mud Puffs.

Might as well say it up front: Mud pots are great because their thick, bursting bubbles can sound like a chorus of rude noises or "greetings from the interior." That's why the few places they're found in Yellowstone are usually surrounded by gaggles of giggling visitors with video cameras rolling. A mud pot is basically just a hot spring where a low water table results in a bubbling broth of water and clay. Hydrogen sulfide also helps to keep mud pots muddy, breaking down chemically (with help from thermophiles) in order to form rock-dissolving sulfuric acid. As heat and gasses escape from below, bubbles in the muck swell and pop, flinging mud chunks onto the banks to form gloppy clay mounds. The mud's thickness varies as the water table changes with the seasons.

The Fountain Paint Pots, mid-gurgle.

Artist Paint Pots

Lower Geyser Basin

West Thumb Paint Pots

YELLOWSTONE NATIONAL PARK

WHAT ARE FUMAROLES?

Take away the water from a hot spring and you're left with a fumarole. Often called steam vents, these noisy thermals occur when available water boils away before reaching the surface. All that escapes the vent is heat, vapor, and the whisper-roar of a giant, menacing teakettle. Fumaroles are often found on hills and scarps. The gases expelled from fumaroles might include carbon dioxide, sulfur dioxide, and hydrogen sulfide. Some features, like Red Spouter in the Lower Geyser Basin, can exhibit different behaviors depending on the seasonal water table, so what's a fumarole today could be a hot spring in a few months.

FUMAROLE FAQs

Word origin? From Latin *fumus* for "smoke."

Also known as? Solfataras, from *sulpha terra*, Latin for "land of sulfur."

Yellowstone's hottest fumarole? Black Growler at Norris, up to 280° F.

How many fumaroles are in Yellowstone? Around 4,000.

Roaring Mountain fumarole.

Lower
Geyser Basin

**YELLOWSTONE
NATIONAL PARK**

TIPS ON EXPLORING

SAFETY TIPS

Don't leave trails or boardwalks in the frontcountry basins.

Stay at least 10 feet away from backcountry thermals.

Keep extra distance in winter in case of unstable snow shelves.

Never (ever!) bathe or soak in a geyser, hot spring, or mud pot.

Never bring pets into thermal areas.

Don't throw or dip any objects into thermal features.

Leave the area if you feel sick or dizzy—it could be overexposure to thermal gases.

Keep an eye on kids and be sure they understand the danger.

LEARN MORE

Geyser Observation and Study Association: www.geyser-study.org.

The Geysers of Yellowstone by T. Scott Bryan.

Windows into the Earth by Robert B. Smith and Lee Siegel.

Microbial Life resources from Carleton College's Science Education Resource Center: serc.carleton.edu/microbelife.

PHOTO TIPS

Set your alarm clock: generally, the best light for shooting the geothermal features is early in the morning. (You'll avoid the thickest crowds then, too.) The runner-up time is the late afternoon.

Breezy days are good for photographing geysers, since the steam will be blown away from the jetting water. But avoid standing down wind or your view can be clouded with steam.

If you get water from a thermal feature on your lens, be sure to dry it off quickly. The water has a high mineral content and can mark your lens.

Taking in the view at Grand Prismatic Spring.

Yellowstone's
Upper Loop

Mammoth Terraces

Travertine terraces like this one at Mammoth's Canary Spring can grow by as much as two feet per year.

Superheated water
pours over the
ledges and tiers of
Canary Spring.

MAMMOTH HOT SPRINGS

WATER TEMPERATURE:
130 to 168°F

ROCK FORMED:
travertine

RATE OF TRAVERTINE ACCUMULATION:
two tons a day

 # MAMMOTH HOT SPRINGS

See the Yellowstone National Park: Upper Loop and Mammoth Hot Springs maps.

A bull elk strides like a general across the lawn of the former cavalry barracks, his bugle call echoing the reveille that once proclaimed sunrise and sunset at Fort Yellowstone. His harem grazes silently among stately stone buildings, where the ghosts of soldiers and settlers mingle with wide-eyed park visitors and rangers directing traffic. Just yards away, the landscape takes on the color and contours of a burnt marshmallow, an otherworldly hillside with pale turquoise pools and rivulets of super-heated water coursing across sculpted travertine terraces. Find the right spot at Mammoth Hot Springs and you can take in this entire panorama with one sustained gaze.

Because the northern reaches of the park lie beyond the rim of the Yellowstone caldera, the region's geological footprint differs from much of the rest of the park. In the absence of the rhyolitic lava flows that helped form most of central and southern Yellowstone, great subterranean limestone deposits still exist in the Mammoth area, and these help to give the hot springs terraces their unique color and character. What's more, the region's nonrhyolitic soil supports a wider variety of plant life, and although much of the low, dry northern range is dominated by sagebrush steppe, stands of aspen and fir can be found in the forested areas, interspersed with the ubiquitous lodgepole pine.

The remnants of Sheepeater wickiups in the forests east of Mammoth evoke the tribe's presence in the area before the arrival of Euro-American explorers. In the mid-1800s, the Shoshone and Bannock tribes began tracing hunting migrations over the Gallatin Range and across the Yellowstone Plateau, forced east by rapidly dwindling buffalo herds in their ancestral territories west of the Continental Divide. Mammoth Hot Springs was an important stop on what has become known as the Bannock Trail, and it's easy to imagine great hunting parties descending from nearby Snow Pass to rest at the sacred springs.

The hot springs were also known to Western fur trappers by the early 19th century, and primitive maps based on their tales identify the spot as "Boiling Spring White Sulphur Banks" and "Sulphur Mountain." By the time the Hayden expedition gave Mammoth Hot Springs a name that stuck, savvy settlers and Montana miners were already using the springs for their supposed therapeutic value. In fact, when the Hayden party arrived at the hot springs in 1871, expecting to find themselves more or less alone in the still largely unexplored territory, they were surprised to discover a small community of blissed-out soakers lounging in a semi-permanent camp at the base of the springs.

Mammoth Hot Springs has the honor of having housed the first tourist accommodation in Yellowstone, a reportedly squalid hotel and bathhouse built in 1871 by a pair of businessmen from nearby Bozeman. Attempts to cash in on Yellowstone's thermal features continued after the national park was established in 1872. The glut of unauthorized commercial activity—along with widespread poaching and vandalism—helped prompt Yellowstone's beleaguered civilian administrators to relinquish control of the park to the U.S. Army in 1886.

Mammoth was an easy choice for the Army's Yellowstone headquarters due to its low elevation and relatively mild winters, as well as its proximity to frontier towns to the north. Today, you can glimpse the Army's legacy at Mammoth in the imposing sandstone structures that make up the Fort Yellowstone Historic District. The buildings continue to serve as Yellowstone's administrative heart, and Mammoth is the only village with a few year-round services, including a post office, a health clinic, and general store. These services, along with those mild winters, make Mammoth the base camp of choice for Yellowstone's cold-weather adventurers.

A bull elk crosses a meadow near Mammoth.

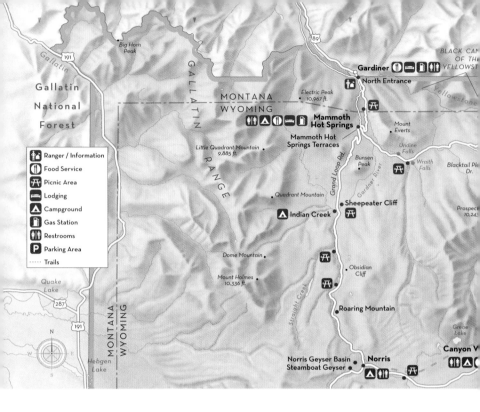

The Springs

The chalky tiers at Mammoth Hot Springs stand out visually among Yellowstone's many thermal areas, but they were formed in much the same way. Though the springs lie more than 20 miles outside of the Yellowstone Caldera, a fault line stretching north from the **Norris Geyser Basin** channels hot water into the porous rock layers below, and water from this scalding subterranean river ascends to the surface via an underground maze of fissures and cracks. Along the way, the water bonds with carbon dioxide, and the resulting acidic solution dissolves minerals as it rises. When the water reaches the surface, a portion of these minerals are deposited, forming the alien terraces and cones of Yellowstone's thermal areas.

Substantial underground layers of sedimentary limestone set Mammoth apart. In contrast to the silica-producing rhyolite found elsewhere in the park, dissolved limestone recrystalizes at the surface to form a gray-white mineral called travertine, and this is the rock that makes up Mammoth's hot springs terraces. Thousands of years of accumulated travertine have given the place its unique look, a

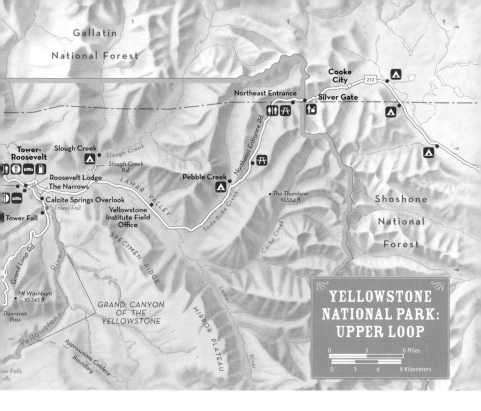

landscape somewhere between an ice palace and an ashtray. Scattered like paint spills across this terrain are the telltale polychrome of thermophiles, the heat-loving bacteria whose algae-like colonies tint the pools as well as their perimeters.

The fickle shifting of the earth continues to affect conditions at Mammoth Hot Springs, and a radiant spring that's furiously churning today might be dry and colorless next month. Check in with rangers at the **Albright Visitor Center** (*see* Nearby Sights, *below*) for updates on recent conditions and schedules of ranger-led programs and tours.

The Mammoth Hot Springs are divided into a Lower and an Upper Terrace. The Lower Terrace is the more compelling of the two, traversed by a winding boardwalk that takes you past a number of fascinating springs. At a good clip, you could stroll the whole thing in an hour, but it's best to take your time. The Upper Terrace is a paved, two-mile road open to cars and foot traffic (but not trailers, buses, or motor homes). You could spare yourself some sneaker tread by taking the car, but you'll be in and out every 500 feet to peer at the springs, so walk if at all possible.

ALBRIGHT VISITOR CENTER

LOCATION: off the Grand Loop Road, near the Mammoth Hotel

TEL: 307/344–2263

Start your Mammoth exploration on the Lower Terrace boardwalk at **Liberty Cap,** a dormant, 37-foot cone that stands like a sentry at the base of the Lower Terrace. During its presumably long period of activity, the pressure below the spring allowed water to reach unusual heights, gradually adding layers to the mineral pillar. Liberty Cap is named for the tapered Phrygian caps that symbolized freedom during the French Revolution—there's one on the seal of the U.S. Senate, too, but it looks more like a hipster beanie. Across the street, **Opal Terrace,** at the base of Capital Hill, is a popular lounging spot for the local elk herds and an equally popular photo op.

Before setting out on the boardwalk, head just north of Liberty Cap and walk west along the path that leads to the Beaver Ponds trailhead. Here you can glimpse **Hymen Terrace,** sometimes overlooked because it's a few steps off the beaten path—and because it goes unmentioned in the park's Mammoth Hot Springs guide pamphlet. The diamond pattern along the terrace's edge takes on some of Mammoth's most vibrant colors when the thermophiles are in full bloom, and during high water periods the water cascades evenly over the honeycombed edges like a Champagne pyramid.

Many of the prints in the Moran Gallery are of landscapes sketched in the field.

The travertine formations of the famed **Minerva Terrace** could be a scale model of a grand cliff-dwelling civilization, its miniature bluffs and escarpments rendered in alabaster and ash. Minerva has cycled through periods of activity and inactivity in the park's recent history, and you'll notice raised boardwalks in some areas nearby, constructed to accommodate rapidly advancing travertine deposits during a particularly active stretch in the early 1990s.

Spend some time examining **Canary Spring,** which makes up much of the broad plateau of the Lower Terrace. Areas in and around the pool retain the sulfur-yellow tinge that earned the spring its name, though brilliant ochre and aqua shades figure into Canary's spectrum as well. Follow the boardwalk to the spring's southeast edge to check out some menacing travertine stalactites where the water spills over a series of tiers.

NEARBY SIGHTS

You're literally taking a step into Yellowstone's past when you walk into the **Albright Visitor Center** (off the Grand Loop Rd., just east of Mammoth Hotel; 307/344–2263), as the building once served as a Fort Yellowstone officer's quarters. Along with a bookstore and a theater, the center has a few historical exhibits and the impressive Moran Gallery,

A former Fort Yellowstone officers' quarters now houses park staff.

a collection of reproduced watercolor paintings by the artist Thomas Moran, who accompanied the Hayden survey on its first park expedition in 1871. If you want to learn more about the red-roofed, double-chimneyed buildings lining the streets at Mammoth, rangers lead daily tours of the rest of **Historic Fort Yellowstone** throughout the summer. One fascinating (and creepy) historic site that doesn't make the tour is the **Kite Hill Cemetery,** where early park employees, settlers, and soldiers lie beneath 19th century headstones and several dilapidated cairns. You won't find the cemetery on the park map, but rangers can tell you what to look for on the hill behind the Mammoth Hotel.

Drive four miles west along the Mammoth–Tower Road to visit two of the park's most accessible and impressive

Thousands of years of accumulated travertine have given the place its unique look, a landscape somewhere between an ice palace and an ashtray.

waterfalls. You'll find **Undine Falls** at a marked roadside pullout, a messy, gorgeous falls where Lava Creek pours sixty feet into a canyon. For a different perspective, drive another quarter mile up the road and park at the Lava Creek Picnic Area just past the bridge. Hike the quarter mile back along the Lava Creek Trail to view the falls from the north rim of the Canyon. Just up the road from the picnic area you'll find the trailhead to **Wraith Falls.** An easy half-mile hike with three gentle switchbacks leads to an overlook where you can see Lava Creek slither down a broad, angled rock face. Wraith Falls is less a thundering cataclysm than a wide brook gone diagonal, and in low water it actually splits into two parallel streams that fall separately and reconnect at the base.

A park visitor eloquently described **the Hoodoos** in 1922 as "a wrecked mountain where giants once played." Not to be confused with the eroded volcanic rocks of Hoodoo Basin in the eastern Absarokas, the Hoodoos south of Mammoth are not true geologic hoodoos, but a collection of travertine boulders wrenched by glaciation and earthquakes from nearby **Terrace Mountain.** There's an extremely short scenic drive 3.5 miles south of Mammoth along the road to Norris, but to walk through the Badlands-esque boulder field, you'll want to hike north a short 1.5 miles along the Howard Eaton Trail, beginning on the west side of the road at the Glen Creek trailhead.

Obsidian was one of the most widely traded minerals among native peoples in early America, and if the smooth volcanic glass set the pre-Columbian gold standard, then Yellowstone was its Fort Knox. Obsidian samples from Yellowstone have been found as far away as Ontario and Ohio, and much of it was likely quarried at the **Obsidian Cliff,** 11 miles south of Mammoth on the Mammoth-Norris Road. Unfortunately, you can't visit the cliffs, as the park service was forced to close the cliffside trails in 1996 after years of tourists breaking off and pocketing rock fragments. You can still glimpse a few obsidian deposits on the east side of the road—be sure to leave them as you find them!

Bright lichens and mosses
stand out like paint splashes
on the ebony rock of Obsidian Cliff.

Sometimes it spits: a hot spring exhibiting geyser-like behavior at the Upper Terrace of Mammoth Hot Springs.

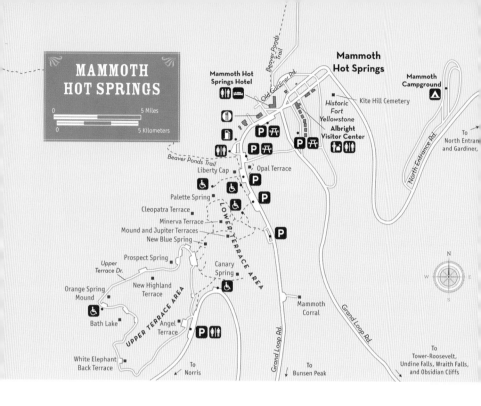

BEST HIKING TRAILS

The **Beaver Ponds Trail** that begins and ends at Mammoth is a gently rolling five-mile loop that leads through a Douglas fir forest and sagebrush meadows sprinkled with wildflowers and aspen stands. Though the marshy ponds that lend their name to the trail are less than spectacular, the solitude is a definite plus for those seeking a break from the bustling Mammoth village. Vistas along the way offer bird's-eye views of the hot springs terraces and the knife-like ridge of Mount Everts. Pick up the trail just south of Liberty Cap along Clematis Creek; it'll deposit you just up the road, behind the Mammoth Hotel.

Haul your hiking boots, mountain bike, or skis to the Bunsen Peak trailhead just south of the cliff-hugging Golden Gate bridge. If it's the vertical you crave, you'll gain 1,300 feet in just over two miles on the **Bunsen Peak Trail** on your way to the domed summit. Take in the views of craggy Electric Peak to the northwest and Mammoth Hot Springs to the north. For a slightly less rugged trip, hike the abandoned **Bunsen Peak Road,** a six-mile unpaved route that curves halfway around the base of the mountain. This route is popular with

YELLOWSTONE'S PAINTER

When Ferdinand Hayden's survey party set out for Yellowstone in 1871, they brought with them a young, informally trained artist from back East, Thomas Moran. Moran had previously done some magazine illustrations of Yellowstone based on explorer Nathaniel Langford's descriptions, but he had no wilderness experience. He went clutching watercolors and a sketchbook and riding with a pillow on his saddle.

Moran proved to be an essential member of the expedition. Throughout the trip, he worked furiously at watercolor studies of features like Mammoth Hot Springs and the Grand Canyon of the Yellowstone. Lat-er that year, Hayden and Langford armed themselves with Moran's work when they lobbied Congress to create Yellowstone National Park. He eventually used his sketches to paint larger, richer oil paintings, including a rendition of the canyon that is now hanging at the Smithsonian.

Moran evolved into a genuine Western adventurer, accompanying John Wesley Powell on a Grand Canyon expedition in 1873 and later exploring the Colorado Rockies with Hayden. Upon his death in 1926, he was considered one of the West's greatest landscape painters.

(far left) The Devil's Slide, Yellowstone, *1871, by Thomas Moran; (center) a photo of the artist; (below)* Grand Canyon of the Yellowstone, *1872, by Moran.*

SURVIVOR: YELLOWSTONE

Yellowstone's first recorded survival story is also its most epic. Halfway into the Washburn party's 1870 Yellowstone expedition, Truman Everts fell behind. Knowing him to be a competent woodsman, his pals kept moving. Then Everts's horse bolted, leaving him on foot and without supplies. He wandered for a month, eating thistles and sleeping near hot springs for warmth. When searchers found him, he weighed 50 pounds, was frostbitten, and half-mad (having crawled halfway across Yellowstone without food or fire). The long, steep mountain east of Mammoth bears his name.

skiers in the winter, and it's one of the few places in the park open to mountain bikers. Because the road snakes back to the Upper Terrace Drive, it's best to make this an out-and-back trip or combine it with the Bunsen Peak Trail to form a 7.2-mile loop. Where the two trails meet, the 1.4-mile **Osprey Falls Trail** descends into Sheepeater Canyon to reach Osprey Falls. The Gardner River dives 150 feet into the gorge here, and the misty nook at the foot of the falls feels like a secret hideout—just you, the falls, and maybe a couple of bighorn sheep peering down from the rim.

For a longer excursion—and some of the most classic and diverse scenery in the American West—the ★BLACK CANYON OF THE YELLOWSTONE is an unparalleled hiking experience. The trail follows the Yellowstone River 18.5 miles through the park's northern range, a remote and largely flat trail that's got a little of everything: mountain views, excellent fishing, a grand suspension bridge, the thundering Knowles Falls, and likely run-ins with elk, pronghorns, and even bears. What's more, if you start your hike at the Hellroaring Trailhead four miles west of Tower Junction, you'll lose more than a thousand feet in elevation and end up in the border town of Gardiner, where you can treat yourself to a huckleberry milk shake.

East of Mammoth, the landscape is dominated by the stunning peaks of the Gallatin Range, and a vast network of long-distance trails provides true alpine junkies entrance to this mountain wilderness. If you came to Yellowstone in search of serious backcountry adventure, few routes pose the challenge, or offer the jagged, high-country beauty, of the 40-mile **Gallatin Skyline Trail.** Well-conditioned and well-prepared hikers can graze the sky as they ascend and descend multiple mountain passes, topping out near 10,000 feet above sea level at the lordly Big Horn Peak.

OTHER ACTIVITIES

You won't find ★BOILING RIVER on your park map, but that doesn't mean it won't be crowded when you get there. This spot where nearby hot springs pour into the Gardner River lures soakers from mid-summer onward. The rare park-sanctioned frontcountry soak is found a half-mile upstream from the parking area near the sign marking the 45th parallel along the North Entrance Road. Naturists should seek their baths elsewhere, as this is a strictly family-friendly area.

Horseback riders silhouetted by the sunset.

Mountain biking on Old Gardiner Road, the former stagecoach route between Mammoth and Gardiner, will keep your adrenaline level well within street-legal limits, but you'll have good views of Sepulcher Mountain and perhaps an elk herd nonchalantly following your progress. Auto traffic is only allowed to drive north on the gravel road, and though bikers have two-way privileges, it's a five-mile uphill trip from Gardiner to Mammoth.

The park concessionaire leads hour-long interpretive **horseback rides from the Mammoth Corral** (Mammoth–Norris Rd., between Upper and Lower Terraces), heading south through rolling sagebrush flats toward the looming dome of Bunsen Peak. Make reservations with the Mammoth Hotel or through the Xanterra reservation hotline (307/344-7311 or 866/439-7375).

DON'T TELL ANNAPOLIS

An elaborate wooden map of the United States hangs on the north wall of the **Map Room,** just off the lobby in the Mammoth Hot Springs Hotel. Architect Robert Reamer designed the map during his renovation of the hotel in 1906, and its rich, mosaic-like appearance comes from the sixteen different varieties of wood used to craft it. The hired woodworker's skill is evident in the precise cut of the map's 2,544 pieces, but so is his imperfect grasp of geography—Baltimore is wrongly identified as the capital of Maryland.

In winter, check out a free pair of skates from the front desk at the Mammoth Hotel and hit the ice at the **Mammoth Hot Springs ice rink** out back. Holiday tunes trumpet from a PA and a fire roars on the edge of the rink—BYO chestnuts.

WHERE TO EAT

Mammoth Hot Springs Hotel Dining Room. The green-and-burgundy art deco interior of Mammoth's main restaurant is almost enough to keep you from gazing out the large windows at the graceful hump of Capitol Hill. Ignore the menu headings taken from the bad chain restaurant playbook (no dessert list should ever come with the title "Perfect Endings") because the kitchen can impress at dinner, especially with regional fish and a bison brat entrée that puts a clever Western spin on British bangers and mash. You can only make reservations in the off season, so in summer you should get here early for a table. Breakfast and lunch choices are less exciting. *Mammoth Hot Springs; 307/344-7311 or 866/439-7375.* **$$–$$$**

Mammoth Terrace Grill. The counter-service grill that adjoins the dining room at Mammoth is your basic fast food–style budget option, good for a quick bite or for the moment when a greasy burger craving gets the best of you. They also scoop a mean ice cream cone. *Mammoth Hot Springs; 307/344-7311 or 866/439-7375.* **$–$$**

 TOWER-ROOSEVELT *See the Yellowstone National Park: Upper Loop and Tower-Roosevelt maps.*

It's fitting that the northeast corner of Yellowstone hosts the Old West–themed Roosevelt Lodge, since in many ways, this region of the park embodies the qualities we attribute to the Western frontier. It's rugged and picturesque, home to robust trout streams and framed by the hackly skyline of the Absaroka Range. It's also comparatively empty,

Lamar Valley is one of the most reliable places in the park to **spot bison year-round.**

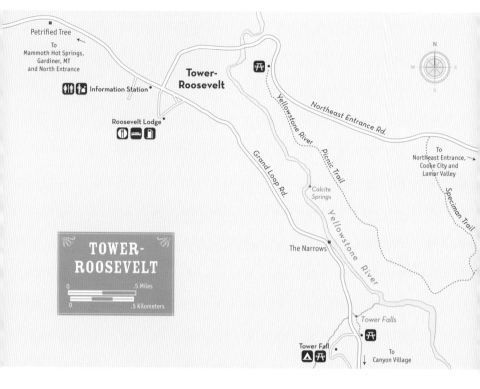

Petrified Tree

To
Mammoth Hot Springs,
Gardiner, MT
and North Entrance

Information Station

Tower-
Roosevelt

Roosevelt Lodge

Yellowstone River

Northeast Entrance Rd.

To
Northeast Entrance,
Cooke City and
Lamar Valley

Grand Loop Rd.

Picnic Trail

Calcite
Springs

Yellowstone River

Specimen Trail

**TOWER-
ROOSEVELT**

0   .5 Miles

0   .5 Kilometers

The Narrows

Tower Falls

Tower Fall

To
Canyon Village

attracting just a fraction of the visitors who make the pilgrimage to Old
Faithful or Canyon. Many come just to glimpse the regal Tower Falls,
leaving the rest of the region as lonesome as a cowboy campfire ballad.
Roosevelt itself is a midsized village, with the lodge, a general store, and
a gas station, but not much else.

*The frosted face
of a bison is one
of the park's most
iconic images.*

Yellowstone's northeast corner has long been something of a hin-
terland, far enough from the park's first nerve centers at Mammoth,
Norris, and Old Faithful that early administrators had trouble
fending off squatters. Early exploration of Lamar Valley and the
Absarokas fell to the miners and prospectors searching for gold
there in the mid-1800s. When they discovered it in 1870, Lamar
Valley became an important supply route to the burgeoning, rough-
and-tumble mining town of Cooke City, then known by the charm-
ing moniker "Shoo-Fly."

LAMAR VALLEY

Low elevation makes Lamar an important wintering range for bison
and elk, and in the spring, wildlife watchers line up to see the herds'

TEDDY IN YELLOWSTONE

As a cofounder of the conservation-minded Boone and Crockett Club, Theodore "Teddy" Roosevelt was an active advocate for Yellowstone throughout his political career. Among other things, he used his influence as President to help end the practice of exterminating cougars in the park. Roosevelt's visit in 1903 prompted Yellowstone's first bona fide media circus. One reporter even attempted to get a scoop on the President's visit by stalking his party through the backcountry, but cavalry rangers discovered him and gave him the boot. Years later, in his autobiography, Roosevelt would recall his wildlife encounters on that trip, writing, "In Yellowstone, the animals seem always to behave as one wishes them to!"

Theodore Roosevelt (left, with the wide-brimmed hat) at Mammoth Hot Springs in 1903.

frolicking new arrivals. The valley is one of the most reliable places in the park to spot bison year-round. It's the site of the Rose Creek Buffalo Ranch, where the park managed a semi-domesticated herd from 1907 to 1952, and which today serves as the campus for the non-profit Yellowstone Institute.

The valley is also home to several competing wolf packs, including Yellowstone's infamous Druid Pack, once the world's largest and still one of the most frequently spotted from along the Northeast Entrance Road. This 30-mile route is breathtakingly beautiful; you should take advantage of its frequent pullouts, especially if you're a wildlife-watcher.

Nearby Sights

Viewed from across a yawning canyon and surrounded on all sides by menacing, hundred-foot stone sentinels, **Tower Fall** comes at you like something out of *Lord of the Rings*. The 132-foot cascade just south of Tower Junction, where the Northeast Entrance Road meets the Grand Loop, would be impressive even without the massive eroded rock columns that inspired its name. A paved trail leads 200 feet down from the lookout to the floor of the Grand Canyon. (From down there you'll have a good view of the imposing canyon walls, but you can't glimpse the falls.) The Yellowstone General Store at Tower Fall draws a crowd, as it's one of few places for groceries and supplies in the northeast corner of the park.

A mile north of Tower Fall is the small and usually crowded parking lot for the **Calcite Springs Overlook.** A short boardwalk loop leads to views of **The Narrows** section of the Grand Canyon, where rapidly cooling lava from an ancient volcanic flow formed the columnar basalt formations that give the far canyon wall the look of a medieval fortress.

Fifty million years ago, in the aftermath of one of Yellowstone's powerful volcanic eruptions, mud and ash swallowed the tree that now sits 1.5 miles west of Tower Junction. Silica particles clogged air pockets in the tree's bark, trunk, and root systems, hardening and preserving the tree in remarkable detail. Just over a century ago, this **Petrified Tree** was put behind a big iron cage—a move that seems unnecessary until you learn there were once *two* petrified trees at this site. Vandals carried away all evidence of the second in the early 1900s. Though the fence prevents close inspection of the remaining fossilized trunk, you can clearly admire the gnarled and knotty texture of the preserved bark. This roadside attraction is just one of

Tower Fall was almost named Minaret Fall—until it came out that the namer had a girlfriend named Minnie Rhett.

The petrified trees that dot Specimen Ridge include sequoias and other species that haven't grown in Yellowstone for millenia.

hundreds of petrified specimens scattered throughout the park's northeast corner. (For a much closer look at Yellowstone's petrified trees, and a much tougher trip, *see* Best Hiking Trails, *below*.)

BEST HIKING TRAILS

Few Yellowstone hikes as gentle as the **Yellowstone River Picnic Area Trail** offer as much solitude or such an abundance of spectacular scenery. This 3.7-mile loop begins at the picnic area trailhead one mile east of Tower Junction and starts by ascending a mellow 200 feet up a sagebrush hillside to the rim of the Grand Canyon. And that's it for elevation gain. The rest of this two-hour amble is a lovely series of canyon overlooks, wildflower explosions in late spring and summer, and Absaroka mountain vistas. Glacial erratic boulders strewn around the trail make fine playgrounds for troupes of yellow-bellied marmots, so keep an ear cocked for their high-pitched chirps and whistles.

Tough out the first 1.5 miles of the **Pebble Creek Trail,** a steep 900-foot climb beginning across the road from the Warm Creek Picnic Area, just west of the Northeast Entrance. The ensuing 10.5 miles more than compensate, descending gradually through lupine-perfumed meadows (and a handful of agreeably brisk stream crossings). Colonies of marmots chum it up with you at picturesque backcountry campsite 3P1, perfectly situated on the creek banks beneath the imposing flat-top of 10,404-foot Barronette Peak. The trail winds up at Pebble Creek Campground, an eight-mile shuttle from the trailhead.

Yellowstone's through-the-roof wow factor comes in part because its most astonishing features are all relatively easy to access. Not so in the case of the ★PETRIFIED FOREST, a cathedral-like plot of millennia-defying trunks that's something of a hidden Yellowstone gem. This astonishing frozen grove can be reached only after a grueling climb in a remote section of the park. Mountain man and world-class exaggerator Jim Bridger once famously recalled a visit, describing a land of "peetrified trees a-growing with peetrified birds on 'em a-singing peetrified songs."

A SMITTEN TRAPPER

"I almost wished I could spend the remainder of my days in a place like this, where happiness and contentment seemed to reign in wild romantic splendor, surrounded by majestic battlements which seemed to support the heavens . . . ."

—Trapper Osborne Russell, writing in his journal after first seeing Lamar Valley in 1835

Blobs of lava hardened to form the columnar basalt cliffs that line sections of the Grand Canyon of the Yellowstone.

You may not spot any calcified birds, but on this silent hillside you'll find dozens of cold stone trees standing within a still-living forest. Begin at the unmarked trailhead just west of the Lamar River Bridge on the Northeast Entrance Road. An old service road leads through 300 feet of sagebrush flat to a trail on the right. The out-and-back trail immediately begins climbing a steep forested hill, and it only stops climbing 1.5 miles and 1,200 feet later, where an immense petrified redwood stump welcomes you to the fossil forest. On the well-defined network of social trails clinging to the slopes below, fossilized wood chips littering the ground are almost indistinguishable from the rocks, and you can peer down into the Lamar Valley at entire constellations of bison.

OTHER ACTIVITIES

Stagecoach and horseback rides are popular activities at Roosevelt Lodge.

The Old West is new again at Roosevelt, and the **Roosevelt Corral** (307/344–7311 or 866/439–7375) just east of the lodge is a hopping equine headquarters in the summer. One-hour horseback rides lead pack trains north through the sagebrush flats of Pleasant Valley, where the toothlike ridge of Hellroaring Mountain rises behind Garnet Hill's gentler forested bump. If you sign up for the two-hour option, you'll hear a chorus of croaks while detouring around marshy Lost Lake.

Feeling saddle-shy? Daily **stagecoach rides** take guests on an hour-long trip in replicas of what once passed for mass transit in Yellowstone. The bright yellow coaches are covered, the benches padded, and the high, spare scenery is spaghetti-western perfect.

Each of these horse-powered trips can be combined with the immensely popular ★OLD WEST DINNER COOKOUT (307/344–7311 or 866/439–7375), a family-friendly cowboy grubfest served three miles north of the village beneath a canvas awning in a high-country meadow. This is ranch-hand chow—thick ribeyes and cornbread—and the sound of forks scraping tin plates is accompanied by a crooning cowboy balladeer. The cookout site was once the grounds of the Pleasant Valley Hotel and saloon, a rough-and-tumble and only quasi-legal establishment opened by longtime park squatter "Uncle" John Yancey in 1884. Much of the property burned to ground in 1906, but your wranglers can spin a few tales about the backcountry hotelier known to brag that his whiskey glasses had never seen a drop of water. Last-minute seats on the stagecoach are usually available, but trail rides to the rain-or-shine cookout should be booked months in advance.

"'Twas but a slough," is how one prospecting scout wrote off the shallow, meandering waters of **Slough Creek** in 1867. His party sought gold, but today the river is filled with anglers seeking the fat and wily trout that have made it a world-famous cutthroat stream. Slough Creek Road provides access to the creek six miles east of Tower Junction, off the Northeast Entrance Road, and the river-following trail at Slough Creek Campground extends another eleven miles to the park boundary. The trail is actually a wagon road providing nonmotorized access to a guest ranch north of the park, so foot travel is easy. In fact, access is so easy and the **fishing** so good that hordes of fly fisherman must compete for space in the prime months of July and August. Midsummer mosquitoes and deerflies make a wade in Slough Creek torturous, but the lurking 22-inch trout are a powerful lure.

WHERE TO EAT

Roosevelt Lodge Dining Room. Just because you're pausing to eat is no reason to get out from among Yellowstone's towering pines. The bark-and-all trunks serving as pillars in the Roosevelt Dining Room complement the organic feel of the room's hardwood floor and fieldstone fireplace. Speaking of organic, some of the best menu items here have a distinctly granola-ish feel, like the vegan-friendly tofu breakfast burrito. All the same, Teddy wouldn't have touched tofu, and the bulk of the menu is cowboy chow, like smoky-sweet barbecue, fried chicken, and knockout baked beans so loaded with beef and bacon they eat like a meal. Bully. *Roosevelt Village at Tower Junction; 307/344–7311 or 866/439-7375.* **$–$$$**

BACKCOUNTRY 101

The cluster of cabins sitting in the sagebrush halfway up Lamar Valley is the humble field campus of the Yellowstone Institute. The Institute is the educational arm of the nonprofit Yellowstone Association, which funds a variety of park endeavors with privately raised donations and proceeds from its bookstores throughout the park.

The breadth of courses offered by the Institute during any given season is almost dizzying. In summer, some hundred different Field Seminars ($100—$400) bring guests together with biologists, historians, and other experts for one- to four-day classes at either the Lamar campus or park lodges. Topics range from waterfowl migration to native history to sculpting, while a smaller catalog in winter might include first aid and tracking classes. Lodging & Learning Programs ($550—$1,900) offer lodge stays combined with more active days spent delving into wildlife and geography topics. Dedicated wilderness students might consider the Backpacking Courses ($400—$1,000), on which small groups, led by both wilderness guides and interpretive specialists, trek through some of the park's far-flung regions. There are several options that are fun for both adults and kids.

CANYON VILLAGE

See the Yellowstone National Park: Upper Loop and Canyon Village maps.

It's a long way down.... Peering over the brink of the Lower Falls.

Following his first glimpse of the vast Grand Canyon of the Yellowstone in 1869, early Yellowstone explorer David Folsom wrote, "Language is inadequate to convey a just conception of the awful grandeur and sublimity of this masterpiece of nature's handiwork." Folsom's "awful grandeur" still permeates the canyon—it echoes as river-roar off thousand-foot cliffs tinged with ochre and henna, it rides the same spiraling air currents that cradle a wing-wet osprey, and it shimmers in the backsplash mists that obscure the base of the Lower Falls like a silver-sequined skirt.

Canyon is the second most-visited area of the park, behind Old Faithful, and its history as a tourist destination is as colorful as the rocks lining the V-shaped slopes. A plot just upstream from the Upper Falls hosted one of the park's first "tent hotels" beginning in 1883. In the 1890s, park administrators and concession companies considered installing a massive elevator to transport guests from the lip of the canyon to the base of the Lower Falls—a proposal that was blessedly abandoned. The first Canyon Hotel was erected in 1891, and parts of that structure were incorporated twenty years later into the "new" Canyon Hotel, a grand Prairie-style lodge designed by unofficial park

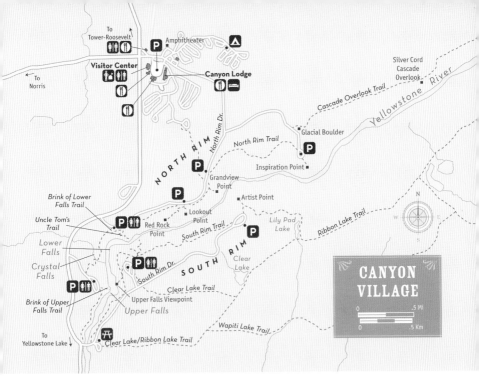

architect Robert Reamer. Few demolitions in the park have prompted as much bitter controversy as when the popular but structurally unsound Canyon Hotel was razed in 1959. Its replacement, today's Canyon Village, is a squat, bustling, and almost suburban spread with a full range of visitor services.

Fifteen miles upstream from the canyon is the mouth of Yellowstone Lake, where ice dams once repressed the flow of the Yellowstone River during the last glacial period. As the ice age waned, the dams gave way, releasing torrents of water that flooded and charged downriver toward the current-day canyon area. The rock in this region is volcanic rhyolite, deposited by a lava flow about 480,000 years ago. The area is also hydrothermally active, and the heat and gases from the thermal basins soften and weaken the rhyolite, making it particularly susceptible to erosion. When the furious waters released by the ice dams struck this hydrothermally enfeebled rock, they carved out the massive canyon we recognize today.

The canyon remains an active hydrothermal basin—you can spot steam plumes and geyser spouts here and there from the rim—and it continues to be slowly eroded by the Yellowstone River. Oxidized iron lends the cliff faces their burnt orange, red, and yellow tones. The canyon extends for 20 miles, descending 1,200 feet at its deepest and ranging from 1,500 to 4,000 feet across.

THE FALLS

The Upper and Lower Falls of the Yellowstone River mark the edge of the region's hydrothermal activity. Where normally erosion-resistant rhyolite from the Canyon lava flow meets up with softer, hydrothermally altered rock, the river has carved the two massive falls that rank among Yellowstone's most recognizable landmarks. The 308-foot **Lower Falls** is the taller of the two, and easily the most photographed. Though spectacular in any season, the water volume is at its highest in the spring. You have a choice of observation points along the North Rim and South Rim drives. Bring binoculars to glimpse osprey nests in the adjacent cliffs and active geysers at the foot of the falls.

Gravity seems to tug a bit more insistently here, as you watch more than 37,000 gallons of water careen into the canyon each second.

The first observation point you reach along the one-way North Rim Drive is **Inspiration Point,** a mile southeast of Canyon Junction. The 15- by 15-foot concrete slab is surrounded by chain-link fence at the end of a short flight of concrete stairs. The view is fantastic, as you can see the Lower Falls peeking from behind a bend in the canyon. Being trapped in a concrete box with 25 other sightseers, however, is less than inspiring. You might seek this inspiration in the evening when it's less crowded. To the west, **Grandview Point** and **Lookout Point** are much roomier and similarly picturesque. Each of these has a bit of a scenic drawback, though. Grandview lacks a view of the falls, and Lookout's canyon view is less stellar than that at Inspiration Point.

★**RED ROCK POINT,** next to Lookout Point, may be the best place to glimpse the Lower Falls. It's a long walk down on a series of paved switchbacks, but from the lower vantage point, the canyon seems to open up around you in a way that it doesn't elsewhere. You'll feel like you're in an encompassing bowl rather than a crevasse. Plus, the steep walk deters many folks from making the trip, so you can be all alone here when the other lookouts are packed. You'll be closer to the rushing water and looking up at its dizzying height.

At the **Brink of the Lower Falls,** about half a mile west of Red Rock Point, experience the singular rush that comes from breathtaking

The classic view of the Lower Falls of the Yellowstone River. At 308 feet, the waterfall is twice the height of Niagara.

PEOPLE IN THE PARKS: LINDA YOUNG, RANGER

Now Yellowstone's chief of interpretation, Young spent 30-plus years working in the park, including stints as a seasonal interpreter and a curator.

Brian Kevin: In the visitor education centers, how do you balance the need for thorough information about complex scientific concepts with the need to explain those ideas to people like me?

Linda Young: We know first of all that when people come to the park, they want to be *in* the park, so we don't develop visitor centers to replace the real experience. You design exhibits to key in on one or two key ideas. You use a lot of visuals, maybe some kind of verbal presentation, since people learn differently.

BK: Love the Yellowstone podcasts on iTunes. Is Yellowstone going digital?

LY: It's important to be able to explore the park from a distance. Live streaming webcams at Old Faithful Geyser—we're so excited by that. Some people leave their browser open all day to watch the geysers. We're also experimenting with some live-streaming ranger programs.

BK: Bad news—Monday will be the next cataclysmic eruption of the Yellowstone volcano. How do you spend your last few days in the park?

LY: Pulled over in the middle of Hayden Valley in the summertime where there are vast herds of bison. Watching them rolling and dusting themselves or wading through the river—it's just sort of mesmerizing, I think.

scenery cut with impending doom. The easily tired and vertigo-prone might avoid the 600-foot descent (in less than a mile) that takes you within spitting distance of the falls' lip. Gravity seems to tug a bit more insistently here, as you watch more than 37,000 gallons of water careen into the canyon each second.

On South Rim Drive, off Canyon–Lake Road, two points give particularly awesome views of the Lower Falls. **Uncle Tom's Trail** (.5 mi off Canyon–Lake Rd.) takes you down 500 feet, inside the deafening roar and dampening spray at the foot of the falls. The paved grades and 300-plus stairs beat the early 20th-century alternative, though, when tourists reached the lookout via rope ladder. ★**ARTIST POINT** (end of South Rim Drive) draws crowds for its easy accessibility and its jawdropping view of the canyon and falls. This perspective prompted the artist Thomas Moran to famously declare the area "beyond the reach of human art." He gave it his best shot, though, and the resulting oil painting hangs prominently at the Smithsonian Museum.

The **Upper Falls** suffers from the same inferiority complex as the painting hanging beside the *Mona Lisa*. If it were located anywhere other than Yellowstone, the majestic 109-foot falls would draw busloads of tourists. As it happens, you might find yourself alone at either of the Upper Falls overlooks, free to contemplate the cascade that explorer Captain John Barlow described in 1871 as "the embodiment of beauty." Get the long view at the **Upper Falls Viewpoint** on the south rim (South Rim Dr., just east of Chittenden Bridge) or the extreme close-up at the **Brink of** the **Upper Falls** (just off Canyon–Lake Rd., .5 mi south of Canyon Junction) on the north rim.

The canyon overlooks are accessible sans car via the three-mile **North Rim Trail** and the 1.75-mile **South Rim Trail.** These two flat trails parallel the roads and are partially paved. You can hop onto them at several points, but an easy place to access either one is at Chittendon Bridge. Only from the North Rim Trail can you glimpse the hush-hush "third falls." **Crystal Falls** dives 129 feet in an elegant triple cascade about halfway between the two "brink" overlooks. On the trail just above the falls is a fascinating spot where Cascade Creek plunges in and out of a small cave. Cautious and sure-footed hikers can shimmy about 20 yards down a barely visible spur trail for a closer look.

NEARBY SIGHTS

The hands-on multimedia exhibits at the ★**CANYON VISITOR EDUCATION CENTER** (307/242-2550) do the work of piles of textbooks to catch you up on Yellowstone's complex geologic story. You can easily spend a half-hour just exploring the massive, three-dimensional park relief map, which lights up to illustrate fault lines, glacial routes, and a timeline of the Yellowstone supervolcano's major lava flows. If the cataclysm of a Yellowstone eruption doesn't trip you out, you might try ogling one of the world's largest lava lamps or spinning (yes, spinning) the 9,000-pound granite globe. Completed in summer of 2006, this is one of the parks' most engaging visitor centers.

CANYON VISITOR EDUCATION CENTER

TEL:
307/242-2550

A glacial erratic boulder along the road to Inspiration Point marks the trailhead for the aptly named Glacial Boulder Trail, along which you can spot the **Silver Cord Cascade** on the south rim. Over the course of a leisurely and largely flat mile, you pass several eye-popping canyon vistas, but none compares to the graceful thread of water pouring 800 feet into the canyon from Ribbon Lake. Though it's actually a series of several separate falls, Silver Cord was likely the inspiration for tall tales among Yellowstone explorers of 1,000-foot waterfalls along the canyon rim.

BEST HIKING TRAILS

Three different routes reach the summit of ★**MOUNT WASHBURN,** the 10,243-foot remnant of a mountain range that once stretched 40 miles across the Yellowstone plateau to the Red Mountains near the park's southern boundary. When those mountains literally blew up during Yellowstone's last great volcanic event 600,000 years ago, the result was the 1,500-square-foot Yellowstone caldera—and the killer panoramic views that bring thousands of visitors up Mount Washburn each year. The most popular and least strenuous route begins at **Dunraven Pass,** five miles north of Canyon Junction. The three-mile former stagecoach route gains 1,400 feet as it ascends Washburn's south face, passing through the park's most spectacular and diverse wildflower meadows that peak in June and July. Watch for bighorn sheep, and be sure to take advantage of the telescope in the fire-lookout cabin at the summit.

The campsite cluster at **Sevenmile Hole** represents one of just two opportunities to camp inside the Grand Canyon of the Yellowstone. (The other is far to the north at Agate Creek, where the canyon as neither as steep nor as deep.) It isn't a seven-mile descent into the canyon, though it may feel like it on the way up; the site is actually about seven river-miles downstream from the Lower Falls. Follow the Glacial Boulder Trail from the Inspiration Point road two miles to the Sevenmile Hole Trail, then descend three steep miles into the canyon. The hike up is worth it for a close-up look at the multicolored canyon walls and several backcountry thermal features.

You can walk with the swagger of a genuine wilderness adventurer after a trip along the **Wapiti Lake Trail.** The route begins on the south end of the South Rim Drive, just east of Chittenden Bridge, and ascends gently for 14 miles before steeply dropping off to meet Wapiti Lake at mile 16. But the real adventure begins at mile 15, where well-conditioned backpackers with solid route-finding skills can follow Broad Creek off-trail toward the rainbow-tinged hills and pools of Josephs Coat Hot Springs, five miles downstream near backcountry campsite 4B1. This is a treacherous route, thickly wooded and pocked with unmarked thermal features. The springs themselves are glimpsed by only a handful of people each year—a reminder that the essence of Yellowstone remains thorny and wild.

OTHER ACTIVITIES

Five miles north of Dunraven Pass, the gravel **Chittenden Road** provides a route to the summit of Mount Washburn open to **cycling.** Granted, it takes a semi-masochistic cyclist to appreciate the view and the admittedly fun three-mile descent after the punishing incline of the approach.

If you feel like you're running into the **Howard Eaton Trail** every time you turn around, you're not imagining things. The park's longest trail once meandered its way to nearly all of the villages, though today much of it is unmaintained or off-limits as habitat. The stretch just west of Canyon is good for **backpacking;** it's got shoreline campsites surrounding four high-country lakes. This area is popular for **fly-fishing** and **birding,** too. Marshy Grebe Lake has rainbow and increasingly rare grayling trout, plus whole councils of waterfowl and raptors. You can access the Eaton trail from several trailheads along the Norris-Canyon and Canyon-Tower Roads.

The **Canyon Corral** (Canyon–Lake Rd., 1 mi south of Canyon Junction) leads one- and two-hour **horseback trips** along nearby Cascade Creek. The longer trip takes a route along the shallow but scenic Cascade Canyon, and the views are worth a saddlesore bottom. Make reservations at the Canyon Lodge or through the Xanterra reservation hotline (307/344–7311 or 866/439–7375).

Where to Eat

Canyon Lodge Dining Room. Some parts of the distinctly 1950s-style Canyon development have aged better than others, and where the dated cabins and hokey retro gift shop are village shortcomings, Canyon's lounge and dining room have a Rat Pack-ish vibe. In the lounge, you can sip a huckleberry martini beneath giant, asterisk-shaped light fixtures as embers crackle in the stone fireplace. The dining room's specialty burgers are a good bet at lunch or dinner; try the superb, smokey-sweet salmon burger made with sustainably raised fish. *Canyon Village; 307/344–7311 or 866/439–7375.* **$$–$$$**

Canyon Lodge Cafeteria and Deli. The crowds at Canyon move fluidly and quickly through this clean, bright room. Think egg dishes for breakfast, sandwiches for lunch, and dinner entrées like those in the dining room: chicken, fish, a pasta bar. It's counterservice only at both the caf and the neighboring deli. *Canyon Village; 307/344–7311 or 866/439–7375.* **$–$$**

Canyon Soda Fountain. Just because you're not cooking over a fire pit doesn't mean you can't have a little camp with your meal. The 1950s-style diner inside Canyon's Yellowstone General Store takes the village's Eisenhower-era look and runs with it, serving up burgers and diner-style breakfasts in a room full of neon, swivel stools, and broad Formica countertops. Sure, it's all a little hokey, but the paper-hat-wearing waitstaff serves up the best root-beer float in the park. If Richie Cunningham and the Fonz came to Yellowstone, this is where they'd stop. *Canyon Village; 307/242–7377.* **$–$$**

Spotlight on
WINTER IN YELLOWSTONE

The best reason for a visit to the Yellowstone region between December and March is the opportunity to experience the parks without crowds. There are many intense, unique sensory and sightseeing pleasures, too. The first thing that strikes you about winter here is the quiet. The gargantuan snowpack—as many as 200 inches annually at low elevation—seems to muffle the sounds of bison foraging in the geyser basins and of hot springs simmering. Wildlife migrates into the valleys, meaning elk and bison herds are easier to spot. If you're ready to work up a sweat on a pair of skis or snowshoes, you'll be rewarded with alpenglow in the Gallatin, Teton, and Absaroka ranges that's at its most luminous in winter. In the solitude and silence of Greater Yellowstone's "secret season," even an easy boardwalk stroll feels like an exhilarating journey.

◄◄ Moose Falls, an easy-to-reach spot near Yellowstone's South Entrance.

LANDMARKS TRANSFORMED

It's amazing to see how wind and cold make Greater Yellowstone even more otherworldly. The thermal basins look like factories, as steam pours from geysers, hot springs, and fumaroles. Plants cling to life around the thermals, where heat leaves patches of open ground and melts the snowdrifts into bizarre, Seussian shapes. Cold temperatures send mud pots into slow motion, their bubbles gradually swelling and popping. Heavy coats of snow disguise the familiar faces of the Teton peaks. Smaller waterfalls freeze solid, while giants like Yellowstone's Lower Falls freeze partially, with water cascading over icicles as big as grain silos. Despite its size, Yellowstone Lake ices over completely, becoming a great white snowscape that groans as the ice beneath it shifts.

Air bubbles trapped in lake ice.

As surface ice on frozen lakes changes temperature, it cracks and thrusts up ice slabs called pressure ridges.

Lower Falls

Old Faithful

Yellowstone Lake

YELLOWSTONE NATIONAL PARK

A hot spring pool in the West Thumb Geyser Basin remains unfrozen in winter.

Steam from the hot springs smothers snowy boardwalks at West Thumb.

WILDLIFE SPOTTING

As a rule, animals in Yellowstone and Grand Teton head *down* when the thermometer falls. Herbivores like elk and bison head to the warmer, less snowy valleys to find vegetation; predators like wolves and cougars follow them. As a result, you're more likely to see these animals in the frontcountry in winter than in other seasons, and they're often easier to spot against the white backdrop. Some bison journey west from their rutting grounds in Hayden Valley to forage in the geyser basins. Others move to Lamar Valley and other low areas north of Yellowstone. Elk congregate in a massive herd at the National Elk Refuge outside of Jackson. Keep one eye on the ground as you explore—the snow makes it easy to pick out animal tracks.

Heat-seeking bison in the Lower Geyser Basin.

A looker of a cow elk stops snowcoach traffic in Yellowstone.

The red fox *(top left)* hunts small rodents in winter by listening for them beneath the snow. Its most endearing habit is its pounce, when it dives headfirst into a snowdrift to come up with a wriggling snack. If you're lucky, you might spot the tracks of the elusive, rare lynx *(upper right)*. It's easier to spy the lookalike bobcat. Resourceful otters *(left)* take advantage of thermal ice-melt in the rivers to fish and avoid predators.

GET OUT IN THE COLD

Since motorized travel is limited in Greater Yellowstone during winter, you'll have the greatest range of exploration if you're traveling under your own steam. But in Yellowstone, you can also travel by snowcoach. These coaches have tracks instead of tires to navigate the park's snowed-in roads and are used for both tours and general transportation. The old-school variety, called Bombardiers, are squat, sputtery little things with snug interiors often dominated by the sound and smell of the engine. Newer models are often no more than conversion vans all Frankensteined up with giant skis and tank treads—a more comfortable, if less authentic, ride. Snowcoaches carry passengers in groups of a dozen or so, with drivers acting as chatty guides. Keep your camera handy as you trundle along in these slow-going behemoths.

AERIAL TRAM

Powderhounds cheered when Jackson Hole Mountain Resort unveiled its bigger, faster "Big Red Box" in 2008. The Jackson Hole Aerial Tram traverses the largest vertical rise in North America, ascending by cable 4,139 feet to the summit of Rendezvous Peak—with breathtaking alpine views along the way. It's used by both skiers and sightseers. *See* the Gateway Towns chapter for more info.

One of Xanterra's Bombardier snowcoaches unloads in front of Old Faithful Snow Lodge.

Jackson Hole
Aerial Tram

**GRAND TETON
NATIONAL PARK**

Swooshing through the snow behind a team of sled dogs, you can barely hear their excited panting over the sound of the wind in your ears. Jackson is a mushing capital, home to multiple Iditarod veterans. Though dogsledding isn't permitted in the parks, **Jackson Hole Iditarod Sled Dog Tours** (800/554–7388) and **Continental Divide Sled Dog Adventures** (800/531–6874) lead trips in the nearby national forests.

Snowmobiling in Greater Yellowstone remains controversial, if popular. There are plenty of designated routes in the national forests, but the parks have been embroiled in court battles over snowmobiling inside their borders. (Opponents cite the snowmobiles' noise and pollution.) At this writing, guided trips, with capped speed limits, were offered in Yellowstone and Grand Teton national parks. In the forests, trails give quick access to remote backcountry. Here, a sledder roars along the hills at Togwotee Pass, east of Grand Teton.

Cross-country skiing is the best way to see the parks in the secret season. You'll see the landscape on a more intimate scale, a sense reinforced by the closeness of the winter weather. Snowed-under roads and paved trails make ideal routes for beginner skiers, with the chance of encounters like this one between skiers and bison in the Upper Geyser Basin. Yellowstone is also a backcountry skier's Shangri-La. In Grand Teton, the relatively flat floor of Jackson Hole makes for easy skiing with breathtaking views.

The skis versus snowshoes debate has been raging among winter wilderness junkies for as long as people have been strapping various boards to their feet. Like cross-country skiing, snowshoeing in Greater Yellowstone offers some of the best access to far-flung backcountry vistas. Many people find snowshoeing easier to learn, and snowshoes are arguably better in heavily wooded terrain.

WINTERTIME TIPS

SAFETY FIRST. Admittedly, official safety checklists can be bit overbearing. But in these winter extremes, there's no messing around. The parks' newspapers and the NPS Web site publish exhaustive gear guides and safety tips. Follow them to the letter.

PACK SUNSCREEN. It's 10°F and overcast—why bother with sunscreen? Because UV rays don't take winter vacation, so slather on the SPF. (I learned the hard way by getting a debilitating sunburn while skiing in Yellowstone.)

WARMING TREND. Most structures are shuttered up throughout winter, but Yellowstone maintains a few warming huts with drinks and snacks. Find them at Canyon, Fishing Bridge, Indian Creek, Madison, Mammoth, Old Faithful, and West Thumb. In Grand Teton, the Dornan's complex in Moose keeps some concessions open year-round.

GIVE YOURSELF SOME WIGGLE ROOM. Winter travel to and from Yellowstone and Grand Teton is complex. The closest airports to Yellowstone are more than an hour away, road conditions are volatile, and snowcoach schedules are capricious. Don't time your travels to the hour. Instead, bookend in-park excursions with nights in the gateway towns.

TOTAL PACKAGE. The easiest and most budget-friendly way to stay in Yellowstone's two winter lodges (Mammoth Hotel and Old Faithful Snow Lodge) is to book a single package with **Xanterra** (866/439–7375; www.travelyellowstone.com) or the **Yellowstone Institute** (307/344–2293 ; www.yellowstoneassociation.org). This takes less time and money than separately booking lodging, meals, activities, and snowcoaches.

Hitting the powder.

Yurt Camp

Grand Loop Road

Yellowstone River

YELLOWSTONE NATIONAL PARK

Deep in Yellowstone National Park, outfitter **Yellowstone Expeditions** (406/646–9333; www.yellowstoneexpeditions. com) erects a temporary skiers' community each winter. Yurt Camp is where to find Yellowstone's most intense winter experience, skiing your brains out and relaxing in the yurts themselves, cozy wood-and-canvas structures that serve as camp's cooking, dining, and social areas. The excellent guides lead flexible daily trips and beginners are welcome.

Grand Teton
National Park

Mount Moran reflected in the Snake River at Oxbow Bend—one of the most popular spots in the park for landscape photography.

In summer, entire
meadows of Grand
Teton National
Park explode with
silvery-blue lupines.

Mountain climbers ascending Grand Teton, looking down at the Middle Teton Glacier.

*Sunrise over
Jackson Hole.*

THE SHAPING OF GRAND TETON

Seven thousand feet above the sagebrush flats of Jackson Hole, protruding like a cufflink from a hunk of wind-battered granite, a tiny disk of scuffed aluminum marks the summit of Grand Teton. It was placed there in 1968, anchored into the rock at 13,770 feet by members of the U.S. Geological Survey. In the space where most USGS summit markers note an elevation, Grand Teton's marker is left blank, a reminder, perhaps, that the mystique of Wyoming's second tallest peak comes not from its height, but from the dramatic profile it cuts across the sky. To touch the summit of Grand Teton is a singular feat, but it is equally transcendent to be touched *by* the mountain—by its angles, its authority, and the long shadow it casts over Grand Teton National Park.

The Grand, as it's known, and the similarly impressive peaks surrounding it form the Teton Range, the youngest mountains in the Rockies. The mountains themselves abut the park's western border, with the broad valley of Jackson Hole filling in the rest of the park's 310,000 acres. (It's less than one-seventh the size of Yellowstone.)

Unlike the volcanically formed Absarokas that dominate Yellowstone's eastern skyline, the abrupt rise of the Tetons is the result of earthquake activity. The Teton fault formed this way about 13 million years ago, a crack in the Earth running north to south along

Elk grazing with a
Teton range backdrop.

Sunset over Grand
Teton and the rest
of the Teton range.

the mountains' eastern front. During millions of years of tremendous earthquakes—some prompted by energy from the hotspot—the plate on the east side of the fault slid deeper into the earth, displacing chunks of subcrustal material that then wedged beneath the western plate, forcing it upward. We have this tectonic movement to thank for great views of the Tetons' sharp eastern face; there are no foothills to block the panorama. Over time, the mountains' highest sedimentary layers eroded away, exposing rock types usually hidden deep within the earth. As a result, though the Tetons are the youngest mountains in the Rockies, they're comprised of some of the oldest rocks. The glacial millennia gave the mountains their nips and tucks, carving valleys, chiseling rock faces, and leaving behind the park's signature glacial lakes, each one reflecting the surrounding peaks.

The indigenous groups that hunted and foraged in the Jackson Hole region, notably the Shoshone and Bannock tribes, had fine Dungeons & Dragons–esque names for these mountains, like "The Hoary Headed Fathers" and "The Ghost Robbers." Leave it to the overimaginative and sex-starved fur trappers visiting the region in the early 1800s to have named the central trio of peaks after a part of the female anatomy: "les Trois Tetons," or "the Three Breasts." Thankfully, regional trapper Davey Jackson found his name attached to the diverse and wildlife-rich valley—or "hole," in trapper slang—before his bawdier peers claimed the naming rights.

Grand Teton National Park as it exists today didn't come into being until 1950, more than 75 years after its landmark neighbor to the north. A half-century of settlement prior to national park status has left the valley as rich in historic structures as it is in natural resources. Jackson Hole is characterized by the winding Snake River, by sagebrush steppe, and by stands of pine and aspen, but it is also dotted with turn-of-the-20th-century homesteads, ranches working and defunct, and other relics. As you drive, hike, bike, and paddle through the park, it's worth tearing your eyes every so often from the Tetons' weathered splendor in order to examine the artifacts that make Grand Teton National Park as much a living museum as an outdoor playground.

A grizzly bear claw necklace proved great hunting skill and bravery. Some of the claws on this necklace were taken from earlier necklaces, dating from 1800.

Many of the Native American artifacts at the Indian Arts Museum were collected by the Rockefeller family.

EXPLORING THE PARK

See the Grand Teton National Park and Jackson Hole maps.

When you enter Grand Teton from the north, the shoreline of **Jackson Lake** is a constant companion along the 10-mile drive to **Colter Bay Village,** where a full range of visitor facilities attracts mobs of tourists throughout the summer. At the **Colter Bay Visitor Center** (off U.S. 89/191/287, 5 mi north of Jackson Lake Junction; 307/739–3594) the **Indian Arts Museum** is the primary draw, with its weapons, crafts, instruments, and other items created by Western native peoples. The mandala-like beaded textiles alone are worth the visit, and artists from local tribes occasionally drop in for clinics and demonstrations. The free museum is open throughout the summer and offers daily guided tours of the collection. Ask at the center's info booth about Junior Ranger hikes and other ranger-led programs.

Even when compared to the monuments behind it, Jackson Lake is an impressive sight, a huge swath of blue separating the remote northern Tetons from the roads and services on the eastern shore. A flotilla of boats takes to its still waters in high season. A spur road at Jackson Lake Junction heads east toward Moran Junction and U.S. 26/89/191, what's frequently referred to as the Jackson Highway or Outer Park Road. West of Jackson Lake Junction, where Teton Park Road crosses

the **Jackson Lake Dam,** an interpretive display explains this fascinating and sometimes controversial feature. Though Jackson Lake is a natural glacial lake, the dam—which predates the park by several decades—regulates the flow of water to the **Snake River.** Since Idaho farmers downstream own much of the regional water rights, irrigation demands in dry summers can drain the lake to unsightly levels. Consider it a glimpse into the messy drama of water-rights policy in the West.

South of the dam and Colter Bay, the **Signal Mountain Summit Road** (off Teton Park Rd., 4 mi south of Jackson Lake Junction) presents that rare opportunity to top out on a mountain peak without having to turn off the A/C, though the paved, five-mile route to this isolated 7,720-foot summit is no picnic for your engine (RVs and trailers are prohibited). Two overlooks—one at the summit, the other about three-quarters of the way up—show off the Teton skyline as well the valley's pastiche of forests, grasslands, and buttes. Get an alpine start (that means before dawn) to watch the sun spill into the valley over the mellow Gros Ventre Range to the east.

Continue following Teton Park Road south to reach the glacial blue **Jenny Lake.** Smaller than Jackson Lake and used by far fewer boaters, the lake nonetheless sees a lot of foot traffic on its shoreline. Next to the general store at the crowded visitor area off South Jenny Lake Junction is a modest log cabin that once served as a studio for early park photographer Hank Crandall. It now houses the **Jenny Lake Visitor Center** (Jenny Lake; 307/739–3392), consisting of a small bookstore, a few illustrated geology displays, and a 3-D relief map. It's worth stopping by the humble visitor center to sign up for the 2.5-hour interpretive hike to **Inspiration Point,** a popular daily ranger-guided trek that's limited to 25 participants (*see* Best Hiking Trails, *below*). Mountaineers and those planning backcountry trips can see an even more detailed relief map at the **Jenny Lake Ranger Station** (307/739–3343) just a few yards up the path.

Where Teton Park Road joins back up with the Jackson Highway is the villagelike hub of **Moose,** where the Snake River separates concessionaire-run gas stations, shops, and places to eat from a small post office and the **Craig Thomas Discovery and Visitor Center** (Teton Park Rd. at Moose, 307/739–3399). Dedicated in August 2007, the facility flashes a cool, modern architectural style, including 30-foot windows, a sweeping copper roof, and a courtyard surrounded by a timber-beam colonnade. Inside the airy museum space, wall-sized photo murals and conventional exhibit panels compete

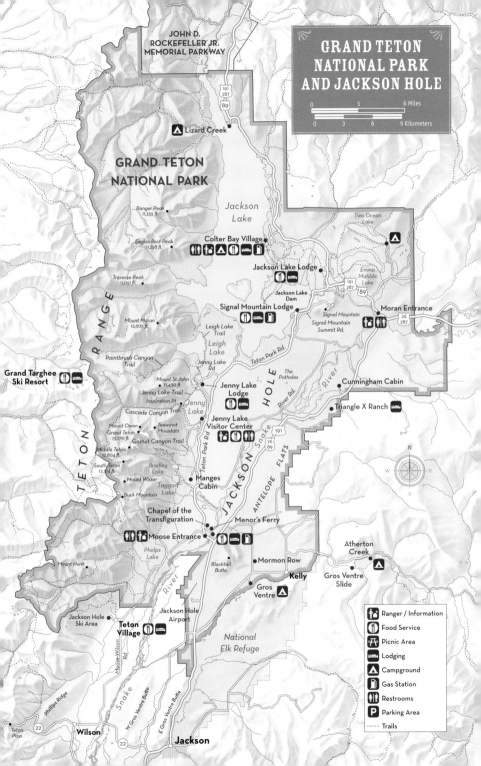

GRAND TETON NATIONAL PARK AND JACKSON HOLE

0 ___ 3 ___ 6 Miles
0 ___ 3 ___ 6 ___ 9 Kilometers

JOHN D. ROCKEFELLER JR. MEMORIAL PARKWAY

191 287 89

Lizard Creek

GRAND TETON NATIONAL PARK

Jackson Lake

Ranger Peak 11,355 ft.

Two Ocean Lake

Eagles Rest Peak 11,258 ft.

Colter Bay Village

Jackson Lake Lodge

Emma Matilda Lake

Traverse Peak 11,051 ft.

191 287 89

Jackson Lake Dam

Signal Mountain Lodge

Signal Mountain Signal Mountain Summit Rd.

Moran Entrance

26 287

Mount Moran 12,605 ft.

Leigh Lake Trail

Leigh Lake

Jenny Lake Rd

Teton Park Rd.

The Potholes

River Rd.

Snake River

Cunningham Cabin

Paintbrush Canyon Trail

Mount St John 11,430 ft.

Jenny Lake Lodge

Triangle X Ranch

Grand Targhee Ski Resort

Jenny Lake Trail

Inspiration Pt.

Cascade Canyon Trail

Jenny Lake

Jenny Lake Visitor Center

191

T E T O N   R A N G E

Mount Owen Grand Teton 13,770 ft.

Teewinot Mountain

Garnet Canyon Trail

26 89

J A C K S O N   H O L E

A N T E L O P E   F L A T S

Middle Teton 12,804 ft.

Bradley Lake

South Teton 12,514 ft.

Mount Wister

Taggart Lake

Cottonwood Cr.

Manges Cabin

Buck Mountain

Chapel of the Transfiguration

Menor's Ferry

N

W E S

Moose Entrance

Phelps Lake

Atherton Creek

Mount Hunt

Blacktail Butte

Mormon Row

Kelly

Gros Ventre Slide

Snake River

Jackson Hole Ski Area

Jackson Hole Airport

Gros Ventre

Teton Village

National Elk Refuge

Phillips Ridge

Moose-Wilson Rd

W Gros Ventre Butte

E Gros Ventre Butte

Teton Pass

22

22

Wilson

Jackson

Legend

- Ranger / Information
- Food Service
- Picnic Area
- Lodging
- Campground
- Gas Station
- Restrooms
- P Parking Area
- Trails

for attention with sexier multimedia elements like floor-embedded video screens that stream, among other things, close-up images of a rolling Snake River. A gargantuan relief model is the best way to visualize the wide scope of the park's topography short of flying over it, and the map lights up to illustrate glacial pathways and wildlife migrations. These arcade-like elements and a smattering of touchable artifacts make the center particularly kid-friendly. Of course there's a staffed information desk and a bookstore; a 150-seat auditorium is scheduled to open in 2009.

Technically, the ★GROS VENTRE SLIDE (Gros Ventre Rd., 2.5 mi east of the park boundary) lies just outside the park's southwest corner, a 20-minute drive from Moose along Teton Park and Gros Ventre roads. The effects of this cataclysmic rockslide, however, were felt throughout Jackson Hole. In 1920 a homesteader named "Uncle Billy" Bierer got nervous about the face of Sheep Mountain over-looking his ranch. "Give it a wet enough year," he predicted, "and all that rock strata will fall down...like a beaver's slickery slide." Uncle Billy sold out, and on June 23, 1925, 50 million cubic yards of rock careened down the mountainside, creating a 200-foot natural dam on the Gros Ventre River inside of a jaw-dropping three minutes. Lower Slide Lake formed behind it within days. Two years later, during a wet spring, the lake burst the top portion of the dam, flooding the river, virtually destroying the town of Kelly downstream and killing six people and countless livestock inside of fifteen minutes.

Twilight at Jenny Lake, a tents-only campground.

It's humbling to read the memorial plaque near the parking area or examine the interpretive displays along the short forested trail. The sure-footed can also pick their way across the boulder field where the river once ran. While the challenge of the parks so often involves comprehending the tangents and arcs of geologic time, the Gros Ventre Slide stuns you with just how quickly entire regions of the map can be forever altered.

Historic Sights

See the Grand Teton National Park and Jackson Hole map.

Cunningham Cabin (U.S. 26/89/191, 6 mi south of Moran Junction) lies on the sagebrush prairie like a coffin, long and low against the horizon. Pierce Cunningham, a former fur trapper who transitioned to ranching in 1888, evidently lived a spartan existence. You can step inside his two-room, sod-roofed cabin and imagine what life was like in this dark, low-ceiling space. Take advantage of the great photo op and a mile-long trail network that wanders across the surrounding prairie.

The classic postcard shot: Moulton Barn on Mormon Row.

YELLOWSTONE AND GRAND TETON NATIONAL PARKS

Built in 1911, the **Manges Cabin** (off Teton Park Rd., 3 mi north of Moose) was isolated, the soil around it poor. When pioneering Jackson Hole homesteader Joseph Manges left to hunt or fish, he hung a sign on the door reading, "If I don't come back, try to make a living off the place." The Park Service has converted the cabin into a barn, but looking west from the Cottonwood Creek Turnout, you can spot the tiny structure looking romantically frail against its mountain backdrop. For a closer look, walk a half-mile north from the signed Taggart Lake trailhead just south of the turnout on Teton Park Road. You'll see the cabin through some trees on your right.

The thick white noise of the rushing Snake River grows louder as you approach **Menor's Ferry** (off Teton Park Rd., 1 mi north of Moose Junction), suggesting what a treacherous ford this would have been before Bill Menor established his ferry service here in 1894.

> When pioneering Jackson Hole homesteader Joseph Manges left to hunt or fish, he hung a sign on the door reading, "If I don't come back, try to make a living off the place."

Rangers operate a replica that takes visitors halfway across the river (as conditions permit). It's a pretty ingenious system, where a platform attached to a river-spanning rope simply aligns itself diagonally against the current, allowing the force of the water to nudge it across.

Up a short path from the ferry, the preserved early-20th-century **Maude Noble Cabin** has a small, fascinating display of historical photographs, dating way back to the bad old days when what's now the glitzy ski paradise of Teton Village was known as "Poverty Flats." It was at the Noble cabin that a small group of locals first convened to discuss pursuing national park status in 1923. Rounding out the historic campus is a stable area with pioneer-era vehicles, a working general store carrying period merchandise, and a preserved homestead, where a chair made entirely from antlers (with points!) hints at a peculiar sort of frontier sadism.

Also found along the short road leading to Menor's Ferry is the **★CHAPEL OF THE TRANSFIGURATION,** an architectural expression of faith that's both poetic and austere. Locals felled the logs and built the tiny cabin in 1925. An aspen stump serves as a pulpit, and behind the altar an unadorned picture window frames the mountains once known as the Hoary Headed Fathers. Only a few muted camera

That's not a painting behind the altar at the Chapel of the Transfiguration—it's a window with a stunning Teton view.

ROCKEFELLER PARKWAY

Named for the philanthropist who helped bring Grand Teton National Park into being, the John D. Rockefeller Jr. Memorial Parkway is a corridor of land between Yellowstone and Grand Teton, adding up to 24,000 acres. Two roads go through this parkway, and seven miles of U.S. 89/191/287 act as a sort of "grandeur buffer zone," a not-always-scenic stretch where southern Yellowstone's lava flows give way to the granite rocks of the Tetons.

The only concession in the Parkway is **Flagg Ranch** (off U.S. 89/191/287, 2 mi south of Yellowstone; 800/443–2311). The former military post and historic dude ranch offers camping, cabins, gas, and groceries. Stop at the adjacent NPS **Flagg Ranch Information Station** (307/543–2327), open in late spring and summer.

Grassy Lake Road runs between Highway 89 and Ashton, Idaho, a narrow gravel route providing access to Yellowstone's Bechler region. The sparsely travelled **Glade Creek Trail** heads south at mile 5 through acres of wildflower meadows, providing access to miles of additional trail in the northern Tetons. **Grassy Lake Reservoir** is just west of the Parkway, a crystal lake popular for stocked cutthroat and shoreline campsites. Note that Grassy Lake Road is lousy for RVs, and it's closed to vehicles from November through May.

clicks break the silence of the sanctuary. The Episcopalian Church of Jackson Hole (307/733–2603 for services) still hosts regular services here in the summer.

As you drive, bike, or stroll down **Mormon Row** in the park's southeast corner (between Gros Ventre and Antelope Flats Rds.), it's hard to imagine how a handful of Latter Day Saints families successfully settled and farmed this remote sagebrush wasteland in the early 1900s. You'll probably recognize the **Moulton Barn** from all the postcards—it's the charmingly dilapidated one with the pointy roofline that mimics the Teton peaks behind it. If you have trouble picking it out, just look where the hordes of amateur and professional photographers are pointing their cameras. The other ramshackle ranch buildings are equally photogenic. All are fragile, though, so you can't go inside. Antelope Flats Road and Mormon Row are closed to vehicles from November through April, but open to skiers and snowshoers.

⊕ BEST HIKING TRAILS

Grand Teton is a hiker's park in a way that Yellowstone is not. More of its summer visitors plan backcountry trips, and there's considerably less backcountry for them to share. The downside of this situation is that absolute solitude is a little harder to come by; the upside is that trails tend to be well traveled and well marked. You're less likely to encounter an unsigned trail junction than in Yellowstone, and marked distances tend to be reliable. Major trailheads into the Teton canyons are clearly marked, mostly along Teton Park and Moose–Wilson roads. Of course, no amount of signage is a substitute for preparation. Always carry a topographic map and a compass in the Teton backcountry, and be prepared for all weather in all seasons in the mountains—snow in mid-August is not at all rare at high elevations.

The smooth surface of **Jenny Lake** gleams with the sort of perfect sapphire blue that makes other blues look plain. You can take it in from every angle along the seven-mile **Jenny Lake Loop.** Head out from the east shore boat docks or String Lake trailhead to encircle this glacial gem, spotting ospreys, grebes, and seasonal wildflowers along the way. Keep an ear cocked for the high, mad yodel of the common loon, often found on Jenny Lake's open water. The trail is flat regardless of which direction you travel, but you'll climb a very steep 250 feet if you opt to take the popular half-mile side trip to the **Inspiration Point overlook** near the mouth of Cascade Canyon An easier-to-reach highlight, Hidden Falls, is at the start of the same spur trail but before the steep climb.

The trail into **Garnet Canyon** from the Lupine Meadows trailhead is a popular alpine access route for climbers and backcountry junkies, so you won't be alone on a day hike or overnight trip there. Still, there are plenty of wildflower meadows and sculpted rock walls to go around. Begin a steady and challenging climb along the Lupine Meadows Trail, reaching a spur trail after three miles that leads to Surprise and Amphitheater lakes, two deep blue pools shrouded in mountain shadows (another 1.6 miles). The trail becomes the Garnet Canyon Trail after the spur, and Middle Teton looms before you for the next 1.5 miles, past the end of the maintained trail and through a quarter-mile of a chunky boulder field leading to ★THE MEADOWS CAMPING AREA. This is the end of the road unless you're planning to summit Grand, Middle, or South Teton. Hemmed in by all three mountains and messy with colossal boulders and snowmelt streams, the Meadows is one of the prettiest backcountry places to pitch a tent in all the West.

Bull elk bugling during the fall rut; several species of blue gentians grow throughout the park.

Although most of the Teton canyons are oriented west-to-east, Paintbrush Canyon runs southwest-to-northeast, so the sun falls on you in unique ways as you navigate the ★PAINTBRUSH DIVIDE TRAIL. The 20-mile loop is one of the park's most popular backpacking trips, a two- or three-day excursion that begins at the Leigh Lake trailhead at the String Lake Picnic Area, off the North Jenny Lake Loop. The initial ascent leads through fields of the bright red wildflower that give the canyon its name. But the flowers are nowhere

In autumn, aspens and willows transform the landscape into a study of colorful contrasts.

PEOPLE IN THE PARKS: "BLACK GEORGE" SIMMONS, VOLUNTEER RANGER

During a 40-year career with the U.S. Geological Survey, "Black George" Simmons led mapping expeditions everywhere from Utah to Liberia. In retirement, he embarked on a second career as a volunteer ranger. Now in his mid-80s, he spends summers in Grand Teton National Park where, among other things, he distributes root-beer floats to surprised and grateful hikers from a ranger station near the Death Canyon trailhead in the southwest corner of the park.

Brian Kevin: Sounds like you run into a lot of people coming on and off the trail.

Black George Simmons: I meet interesting people every year—interesting because of their backgrounds, places they have been, what they do. Perhaps the most fascinating last year was a concessioner restoring the [nearby, historic] White Grass Ranch. He and his wife once spent an entire year crossing the Indian Ocean in their small sailboat.

BK: As a geologist, do you approach Grand Teton differently compared to other places you've worked?

BGS: Not having done extensive study here, my interest is chiefly in being able to respond to visitor questions. It's a terrible thing to have somebody pick up a rock and ask, "What's this?" and then find

yourself unable to identify it! Geologists are never bored when they travel, since they get to try and interpret geologic history from all the passing scenery.

BK: Given all your park experience, do you ever see us making decisions about public lands that we might come to regret?

BGS: Pressure on our wild and undisturbed places is always under progressive increase. Most of the tourists I see are campers, climbers, and hikers—conservationists who are pro-wilderness. Unfortunately, not enough of them are activists who challenge development in Congress and in the courts. If you want to see appreciation for our parks, talk with visitors from Europe, where no wilderness exists.

BK: Let's pretend next week will be another cataclysmic eruption of the Yellowstone volcano. What do you do with your last week in the parks? Where do you go?

BGS: That's an easy one. I'd go nowhere. I'd stay until the last person in the vicinity had been accounted for and was out of the area, and then I'd hang on in case somebody unknown was still there. To fill in the time toward the end, I'd take many, many pictures, which I'd hope could be used later to illustrate the changes that occurred.

to be seen at the 10,700-foot Paintbrush Divide, a rocky and wind-swept ridge where snowdrifts persist throughout the summer. Before descending to Jenny Lake via Cascade Canyon to the south, you'll drop in on two crystal-blue alpine lakes.

➻ ON AND IN THE WATER

The glacial lakes strung like beads along the Teton Fault are as integral to the park's mystique as its conspicuous summits. Sliding across these waters in a **canoe or kayak** is a classic Grand Teton experience. Canoes and kayaks from **Signal Mountain Marina** (off Teton Park Rd., 3 mi south of Jackson Lake Junction; 307/543–2831) or **Colter Bay Marina** (off U.S. 89/191/287, 5 mi north of Jackson Lake Junction; 307/543–2811) have to stay near shore, but Dornan's in Moose lets you take their watercraft farther afield.

Jackson Lake provides, by far, the most surface area to explore, with a number of island-hopping routes in its southern reaches and a handful of paddle-in campsites on its rugged, roadless western shore. The cliffside lake views at the Wilcox Point campsite below Moose Mountain are worth a long day of rowing from Colter Bay. Another great paddle is **Leigh Lake,** accessed via a short portage from **String Lake** along the North Jenny Lake Loop. Named for "Beaver Dick" Leigh, one of the Hole's earliest trappers and a Hayden party guide, the lake entices campers with five isolated campsites and day-trip-pers with stunning views of the pearl-white glaciers on Mount Moran's east face.

In summer a flotilla of sailboats, pontoons, and motor-boats takes to the water at Jackson Lake. It can be crowded near the four boat launches at Colter Bay, Signal Mountain, **Leek's Marina** (off U.S. 89/191/287, 1 mi north of Colter Bay Junction; 307/543–2494), and **Spalding Bay** (Spalding Bay Rd., 9 mi southwest of Jackson Lake Junction), but if you're looking to escape the crowds, head over to the lake's brambled western side, where elk and black bears patrol the shoreline and 11,000-foot crags loom. The smaller Jenny Lake is similarly scenic, though motors exceeding ten horsepower are prohibited. Find the boat ramp on the lake's south shore, off the unpaved road to Lupine Meadows. Signal Mountain has the

★ Cook Your Catch ★

If you bring in a lunker lake trout from Jackson Lake, call the dining rooms at Signal Mountain or Jackson Lodge—they'll usually prepare it for you for a small charge.

Worth getting up early for: sunrise at Oxbow Bend floods Mount Moran in lavender light.

It can be hard to keep your eyes
on the water of Jackson Lake,
with the peaks rising above you.

broadest selection of rental craft, including pontoons, runabouts, and deck cruisers, though you can rent motorboats at Colter Bay as well. Thankfully, Jet Skis are banned throughout the park.

If you're more Gilligan than Skipper, you can still hit the lakes at Grand Teton on several guided trips. Hour-and-a-half-long **interpretive cruises on Jackson Lake** depart daily from the Colter Bay Marina, hooking around small, sylvan **Elk Island** to peek up the canyons on the far shore. Sign on for a breakfast or dinner cruise to lay over on the island for a buffet-style picnic. If you'd rather let the lake winds muss up your hair a bit, Signal Mountain offers one- and four-hour **guided sailboat trips** on which the hum of a motor won't drown out the high, sharp cry of the ospreys. The park's most popular boat rides are the **Jenny Lake Boating Company**'s **shuttles and cruises** (307/734–9227). Named by the Hayden party for "Beaver Dick" Leigh's Shoshone wife, Jenny Lake reflects the 12,000-foot spires of the Cathedral Group. The shuttle runs every fifteen minutes or so in summer, a twenty-minute glide from the dock near the visitor center to the Inspiration Point trailhead on the western shore. Ask at the dock about fluctuating scenic cruise schedules.

Though white water fans revere many of the Snake River's thousand-plus miles for their paddle-friendly froth, the stretch running through Grand Teton is more popular for wildlife-watching joyrides than adrenaline-fueled runs. Most visitors ride the Snake with one of the dozen or so licensed **rafting** outfitters. Most of these—including both park lodging companies—float a speedy but white water–free stretch between Deadman's Bar and Moose, a two-hour trip on which

NOT YOUR AVERAGE PARK

If you flew into Jackson Hole, you probably noticed that you landed directly inside Grand Teton National Park—a truly unique experience because no other national park contains a commercial airport. But then, not many allow hunting and grazing, contain pockets of private land, or allow a massive dam to control the flow of their primary river, either.

Most of Grand Teton's quirks stem from Jackson Hole's having already hosted a small but thriving community when park boundaries were expanded in 1950. The airport and Jackson Lake Dam, for example, predate the current park's boundaries. Strictly regulated hunting and grazing rights were a concession to skeptical locals, guaranteed in the expansion. Today, only a handful of families still have grazing permits, and many people feel the park should phase the permits out altogether.

A few tracts remain privately owned, "grandfathered" in after 1950. The state and county claim roughly 1,400 acres here and there. As if land rights in Jackson Hole weren't complicated enough, there are seven acres near Gros Ventre Junction whose ownership is a mystery.

TETON SCIENCE SCHOOLS

The cluster of pioneer-era buildings squatting northeast of Kelly belongs to **Teton Science Schools** (1 Ditch Creek Rd.; 307/733–1313). Just inside the park's eastern border, the campus was a homestead, a dude ranch, and a hunting camp before the conservation-minded nonprofit took over in 1974. The school runs an always-evolving curriculum of youth and adult education programs, everything from afternoon canoe trips for families ($35) to weeklong resident programs where seniors can study with professional historians and ecologists ($825). Students stay in rustic cabins with postcard-worthy Teton views or in the stylish, eco-friendly dorms on the Jackson campus.

the Tetons loom large and moose sightings are probable. To feel a bit of the river spray, sign on for a three-hour trip with **Will Dornan's Scenic Float Trips** (Moose; 307/733–3699), the only outfitter to run the equally scenic but faster currents between Moose and the town of Wilson. Expect higher water and faster flows in the spring. The calmest Snake waters for do-it-yourself canoeists, kayakers, and rafters are just downstream from Jackson Lake.

As if the Snake River weren't unique enough, it also has its own indigenous trout species, the Snake River fine-spotted cutthroat. The speckly subspecies is prey for crowds of anglers who **float-fish** the Snake after the spring run-off. You can't swing a fly rod in the neighborhood of Jackson without hitting a fishing guide, but **Will Dornan's Snake River Angler** (Moose; 307/733–3699) and the **Triangle X Ranch** (off U.S. 26/89/191, 6 mi south of Moran Junction; 307/733–3699) both lead trips from inside the park. Most of the park's lakes are open to fishing year-round. Jackson Lake is off-limits to fishermen during October, but holds some lunker lake trout for deep-water fishermen. Seasons and regulations in the park are complex at best, so be sure to pick up a Park Service fishing bulletin when you go for your license (*see* the Practical Information chapter).

For swimmers and soakers, the shock of the chilly water in a high-altitude lake is pretty quickly replaced by the weightless calm of floating beneath a mountain skyline. The park's lakes are open to **swimming,** though you'll definitely want to stick a toe in first. Shallow waters and sandy bottoms lure families into the water at the **String Lake Picnic Area** (off the North Jenny Lake Loop). And though it's only truly warm during the hot summer months, the large, gravel-lined pool at **Kelly Warm Spring** (Gros Ventre Rd., 2 mi west of the park boundary) draws a mixed crowd of frolicking kids, tired hikers, and laid-back kayakers practicing their rolls.

⊙➤ OTHER ACTIVITIES

The winged residents of Jackson Hole are far more numerous and varied than their terrestrial counterparts, and birders flock to Grand Teton in all seasons to spot a few of the 300-plus species that have been identified in the area. To get in on the **bird-watching** action, grab a checklist from one of the visitor centers, then head to **Oxbow Bend** (1 mi east of Jackson Lake Junction), a marshy meander where the Snake River turns south out of Jackson Lake. Great blue herons preen in the shallows, hungry eagles dive-bomb the water, and white pelicans visit during spring migration (some even stick around for summer). Other hot spots include **Two Ocean Lake** for waterfowl and **Antelope Flats** for rodent-hunting raptors. Local birding authority Bert Raynes's weekly column in the *Jackson Hole News&Guide* is a must-read for visiting birders. You can find copies of the free paper all over Jackson.

The comparatively flat roads in Grand Teton make the park much better for **cycling** than Yellowstone. In 2008 construction began on a long-debated network of cycling trails to parallel Teton Park Road, Moose–Wilson Road, and U.S. 26/89/191 south of Moose. While that's under way, hit the quiet, mostly paved roads around Kelly and Antelope Flats to hear the elk bugling and smell the buffalo chips. And though the park's hiking trails are off-limits to pedal pushers, the network of unimproved dirt roads is a boon to **mountain biking.** Fifteen gravel miles along the scenic ★RIVER ROAD are flat enough for beginners, with a few small hills for the adventurous. The dusty two- to three-hour ride begins at the Cottonwood Creek turnout and follows the Snake River, showing off the moonlike, kettle-pocked flats known as the Potholes along the way. You'll get excellent Teton views from beginning to end, and the route is refreshingly quiet, as few visitors make their way here. Just east of Antelope Flats, steep climbs and a few singletrack routes on Shadow Mountain attract more experienced riders—follow Shadow Mountain Road north from Antelope Flats Road. The bronzed hard-core riders at **Dornan's Adventure Sports** (Moose; 307/733–3307) rent bikes and dish on other nearby trails.

There are fewer **horseback-riding** options in Grand Teton than in Yellowstone, but many Jackson-area ranches and outfitters lead

(previous page, top) Photographers line up before a bull and cow moose; (previous page, bottom) Oxbow Bend is a great birding location; (this page) a climber hones his chops on Blacktail Butte.

225

AMERICA'S ALPS

The Tetons might rightly be called the birthplace of American mountaineering. The range was considered holy ground by the fledgling mountaineers of the early 1900s, and today the names of the innumerable climbing routes read like a roll call of famous American alpinists.

Grand Teton presented an iconic challenge from the start. Yellowstone's first superintendent, Nathaniel Langford, claimed to have reached the summit with a partner during a USGS expedition in 1872. His sketches and descriptions, though, match a lower side-summit known as "The Enclosure." It's a controversial call, but first-ascent credit generally goes to mountaineer William Owen, who summitted twice in 1898 and launched an aggressive PR campaign promoting his feat.

Exum Mountain Guides (Jenny Lake; 307/733–2297) is the premier guide ser-

vice in the Tetons and one of the best in the world. The group was founded in 1946 by pioneering climbers Glenn Exum and Paul Petzoldt. Petzoldt first climbed the Grand in 1924 at the age of sixteen (while wearing cowboy boots!), and he later founded the National Outdoor Leadership School. Unless you're an experienced mountaineer, a trip with Exum or **Jackson Hole Mountain Guides** (165 N. Glenwood St., Jackson; 307/733–4979) is the best way to look down from the Teton summits.

Rock climbing is equally popular in the park, and both outfitters lead day trips to granite spires and big walls. Beginning climbers might try bouldering in the area known as **Boulder City,** a half-mile northwest of the Cathedral Group Overlook on North Jenny Lake Road.

A climber heading up Grand Teton. Intrepid climbers pioneer new routes up this peak every couple of years.

longer pack trips into the surrounding national forests. The **Jackson Lake Lodge Corral** (off U.S. 89/191/287, 1 mi north of Jackson Lake Junction; 307/543–2811) leads one- and two-hour rides along trails surrounding pine-rimmed Emma Matilda Lake. The **Colter Bay Corral** (off U.S. 89/191/287, 5 mi north of Jackson Lake Junction; 307/543–2811) takes riders on 1.5- and 2.5-hour outings around waterfowl-rich Hermitage Point.

 WHERE TO EAT

★**JENNY LAKE LODGE DINING ROOM.** Without peer in the national parks. Think Gruyère-and-duck-confit croque monsieur as a first course, tender elk medallions as an entrée, and an apricot Bavarian cream dessert. The five-course, prix-fixe dinner menu focuses on wild game and seasonal produce, and changes nightly. Decadent breakfasts follow the same prix-fixe formula, though lunch is an à la carte selection of sandwiches and salads. The space is a terrific contrast between white tablecloths and crystal wine glasses and log-cabin architecture. Men need dinner jackets, everyone needs reservations, and nonguests need high limits on their credit cards (meals are included for guests at the lodge). *Jenny Lake Lodge; 307/733–4647.* **$$$–$$$$**

Mural Room. A moose-shaped butter pat might seem tacky elsewhere, but there's a regal tearoom feel to Jackson Lake Lodge's flagship dining room. Floor-to-ceiling windows frame the northern Tetons; the other eye-grabbers are two massive, stately murals. John D. Rockefeller Jr. commissioned the panels in the late 1950s, and artist Carl Roters delivered the 80-foot-long painting of fur trappers at a Jackson Hole rendezvous. The Mural Room serves all three meals, but the best reason to reserve a table is for a dinner of elegantly plated seafood and wild game. *Jackson Lake Lodge; 307/543–3463.* **$$$–$$$$**

The Peaks Restaurant. Granted, the Peaks dining room looks a little too industrial for its polished menu and high-end prices, but the hot seats are out on the patio, overlooking Jackson Lake and gilded Teton sunsets. This lodge is the park's standard-bearer for organic and sustainable cuisine; the feel-good choices here include sustainably raised beef from local ranches. The efficient servers even hand out little cards explaining the criteria behind their seafood selection. *Signal Mountain Lodge; 307/543–2831.* **$$$–$$$$**

John Colter Chuckwagon. These all-you-can-eat breakfast and dinner buffets are ports in a storm for legions of famished hikers. The buffet table, of course, is done up like a covered wagon, complementing the Stetson-and-wagon-wheel carpeting—it's just kitschy enough to be fun. Table service is quick, with options like omelets and pancakes at breakfast, hot sandwiches at lunch, and steak and pasta dinner specials. Entrées come with bread, salad, and sides (not always the case in the world of park dining), so you'll get your dollar's worth. *Colter Village; 307/543-2811.* $$–$$$

Dornan's has been a Grand Teton institution ever since Jack Dornan started serving burly ranch-hand fare to tourists in 1948. So the old-timey cowboy look and menu are genuine.

★**DORNAN'S CHUCKWAGON.** Dornan's has been a Grand Teton institution ever since Jack Dornan, the son of a Jackson Hole homesteader, started serving burly ranch-hand fare to tourists in 1948. So the old-timey cowboy look and menu are genuine. The dinner ticket loads your plate with all-you-can eat short ribs, baked beans, mashed potatoes, and more. Breakfasts of thick sourdough pancakes and mountains of bacon are glorious; lunch covers burgers and sandwiches. Kids' menus offer scaled-down portions, and the young 'uns tend to get a kick out of eating in the on-site tepees. *Moose; 307/733-2415.* $–$$$

Dornan's Pizza & Pasta Company. This brewpub's dining room (requisite stone fireplace and rustic pine detailing) opens up to two pretty exceptional decks. The rooftop space has a fine Teton view, and the lower deck looks across the Snake River to Menor's Ferry. Sandwiches and salads complement the eponymous entrées for lunch and dinner; many visitors come just to enjoy the bar. The neighboring wineshop is a must-visit, a seemingly incongruous market with 1,600 wines, more than a hundred cheeses, and a wall full of plaques and awards. Get advance tickets for occasional wine tastings at the restaurant. *Moose; 307/733-2415.* $–$$

John Colter Café Court. Under the same roof as the John Colter Chuckwagon, Colter Village's cheaper, counter-service option appeals to anyone looking for variety. Breakfast items include huevos rancheros and bagels, while lunch and dinner run the gamut from burgers, deli sandwiches, pizza, and rotisserie chicken to a few Mexican entrées. The cafeteria gets pretty crowded at mealtimes, but the whole menu is available for takeout. *Colter Village; 307/543-2811.* **$–$$**

Leek's Pizzeria. There's a relaxed cabin feel to this pizza parlor at Jackson Lake's tiny northern marina, where you can dine on the deck when it's nice out and in front of a stone fireplace when it's not. The pizzas and calzones hold their own against anything in Jackson, with largely organic ingredients and creative specialty pies like the Thai chicken with peanut sauce and sprouts. A semiweekly open-mike night brings in a lot of the young concessionaire staff, and while the talent is hit-or-miss, the music keeps things relaxed and fun. Reasonably priced draft beers don't hurt any either. *Off U.S. 89/191/287, 1 mi north of Colter Bay Junction; 307/543-2494.* **$–$$**

Pioneer Grill. What you see is what you get at this 1950s-style, counter-service soda fountain and burger joint. It scores points with families for affordability, a children's menu, and a kid-pleasing, swivel-chair decor. If you're not impressed with the grease scent or luncheonette layout, grab a bison burger from the takeout window, then mosey out to the cathedral-like lobby or patio for better views and fresh air. *Jackson Lake Lodge; 307/543-3463.* **$–$$**

The Trapper Grill. Anyone who's decidedly not an early bird should take note that the Trapper Grill serves breakfast until noon. The menu isn't as overtly green as the one at the grill's neighbor, the Peaks, but you'll still find organic veggies, free-range bison burgers, and fair-trade coffee. A mountainous nacho platter with beef and chicken is a longtime favorite of people seeking adventure fuel on the cheap. Though the dining room decor is pretty bland, broad windows and a nice patio show off the lake and the mountains. If you'd rather stare at a fireplace or a flat-screen TV, you can order off the same menu (except at breakfast) in the neighboring Deadman's Bar. *Signal Mountain Lodge; 307/543-2831.* **$–$$**

Blue Heron Bar. This is easily the nicest bar in the park, and it holds its own against a host of Jackson hot spots as well. Local microbrews dominate the taps, including the stalwart Snake River Lager that's been racking up beer awards for years. The chatty bartenders mix a mean cocktail, too, including a handful of sweet huckleberry concoctions. On the pub menu, keep an eye out for the mountain of superb garlic fries. Chatter hangs thick in the bar, but you can find some peace and quiet in a deck chair on the spacious patio. *Jackson Lodge; 307/543-3463.* **$**

Gateway Towns

Sleigh rides at the National Elk Refuge bring you face-to-face with the herd.

⊙→ JACKSON *See the Downtown Jackson map.*

Walking past the Old West storefront facades in downtown Jackson, your shoes clopping against the wooden sidewalk, you can almost picture the dusty frontier settlement that began with a post office in 1897. Look east of Town Square, toward Center Street, and you can still pick out the wide, hip-roofed building that served as the pioneer community's first courtroom, school, and dance hall.

Then you pass the windows at Sotheby's International Realty, your eye catching on a photo ad for a $14 million home: *7 fireplaces, log construction, Teton views.* In just over a century, Jackson has gone from Old West outpost to the New West's swankiest destination town, its whirligig growth spurred almost entirely by the tourist trade. And though the locals joke a bit ruefully about the billionaires displacing the millionaires, Jackson is also a friendly micropolis catering to travelers and adventurers, a seasonal haven with plenty of room for ski bums, dirtbaggers, and family tourists alike.

Because it's enveloped by public-use land and because it's so chock-full of guides and outfitters, there's no place like Jackson to try all sorts of outdoor pursuits. It's a particularly good place for beginners to try sports that are usually the domain of specialists, like paragliding. You can get around gratis on the Southern Teton Area Rapid Transit, or **START Bus,** that runs throughout town on a seasonally variable schedule.

Exploring Around Town

Jackson loves its wildlife art, and a big bronze statue of two elk and a grizzly bear welcomes you to the **Jackson Hole & Greater Yellowstone Visitor Center** (532 N. Cache Dr.; 307/733–3616). Under the sod roof is a smallish wildlife exhibit, an info desk with park passes and permits, a bookstore, and about a zillion pamphlets for Jackson Hole events and activities. The center is useful from a one-stop-shopping standpoint, as it serves as a headquarters for the town's chamber of commerce as well as the Forest Service, the National Elk Refuge, the Grand Teton Natural History Association, and a few other local organizations.

Just up the road, a block of green space in the midst of bustling downtown is technically called George Washington Memorial Park, but you're more likely to hear it referred to simply as **Town Square** (Cache Dr. and Broadway Ave.). At each corner of the block stands one of Jackson's landmark elk-antler arches, each one usually thronged by tourists taking snapshots. The original arches were built sometime between 1953 and 1960 (no one's quite sure, though park signs go with the later date). In 2007 the community began a multi-year mission to replace each of the old, increasingly brittle arches. It took 1,948 shed antlers to rebuild the arch in the southwest corner. The rest are slated for replacement as the town continues to raise money and antlers.

Heading into Jackson from Grand Teton, you'll notice a great stone fortress rising on a butte alongside the highway. The anachronistic ★NATIONAL MUSEUM OF WILDLIFE ART (2820 Rungius Rd.; 800/313–9553) was designed to mimic a Scottish castle. Inside, twelve galleries of stunning paintings and sculptures remind you that for every tacky "howling wolf" dream catcher in Western gift shops, somewhere there's an oil or stone rendering of the animal kingdom worthy of its subject. In Robert Bateman's *Chief*, for instance, a lone bison bull, mid-charge, stares out from a gargantuan canvas with a gaze that's as arresting as any roadside specimen in Yellowstone. The museum's emphasis is on Realist and Romantic works from the

JACKSON HOLE VISITOR CENTER

LOCATION: 532 N. Cache Dr.

TEL: 307-733-3616

An antler arch gleams with holiday lights at Jackson's Town Square.

The design of the Museum of Wildlife Art is meant to complement the setting atop East Gros Ventre Butte.

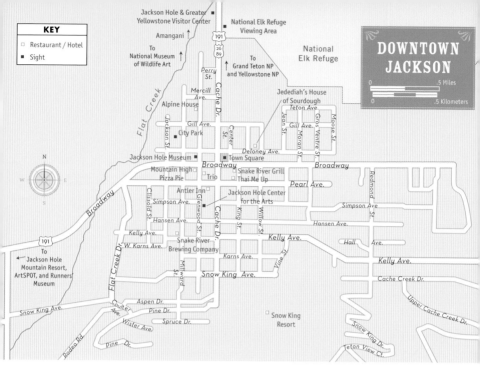

Jackson Hole & Greater
Yellowstone Visitor Center
Amangani ↑

National Elk Refuge
Viewing Area

191
26
89

To
National Museum ↑
of Wildlife Art

↑ To
Grand Teton NP
and Yellowstone NP

National
Elk
Refuge

Perry
St.

Cache Dr.

Mercill
Ave.
Alpine House

Jedediah's House
of Sourdough
Teton Ave.

DOWNTOWN
JACKSON

0   .5 Miles

0   .5 Kilometers

Gill Ave.
City Park

Jackson St.

Center St.

Jean St.

Moran St.

Gill Ave.

Gros Ventre St.

Moose St.

Jackson Hole Museum ■

■ Town Square

Deloney Ave.

Mountain High ☐
Pizza Pie

Broadway
☐ Trio

Broadway

Snake River Grill
☐ Thai Me Up

Pearl Ave.

Redmond St.

Broadway

Antler Inn ☐

Simpson Ave.

Jackson Hole Center
for the Arts

King St.

Willow St.

Simpson Ave.

Glenwood St.

Cache Dr.

Hansen Ave.

Hansen Ave.

Cissold St.

Kelly Ave.
W. Karns Ave.

Snake River ☐
Brewing Company

Kelly Ave.

Vine St.

Hall   Ave.

Kelly Ave.

Cache Creek Dr.

Karns Ave.

Millward St.

Snow King Ave.

Flat Creek Dr.

Upper Cache Creek Dr.

Aspen Dr.

Pine Dr.

Spruce Dr.

Coulter Ave.

Wister Ave.

Rodeo Rd.

Pine Dr.

☐ Snow King
Resort

Snow King Dr.

Teton View Ct.

191
To
← Jackson Hole
Mountain Resort,
ArtSPOT, and Runners'
Museum

Snow King Ave.

Broadway

Flat Creek

American West, but its past exhibits have included provocative artists like Andy Warhol and Georgia O'Keeffe.

Northeast of town, the 25,000-acre **National Elk Refuge** provides a winter home for around 7,500 elk from Jackson Hole and southern Yellowstone. Cut off from historical southern wintering ranges when Jackson began to swell in the early 1900s, the elk are fed alfalfa pellets during their winter stay. Their life is far from cushy, though. Not only is the refuge open to regulated hunting in the fall, but nearby wolf packs are known to cruise the area like hungry diners scanning a buffet table. Horse-drawn **sleigh rides** through the refuge leave from the Jackson Hole Visitor Center between mid-December and late March. Make a late afternoon trip early in the season to scan the shaggy lot as the sun dips behind the Tetons. In summer, megafauna are sparse, but you can drive into the refuge to tour the **Miller House,** a century-old, two-story log manor sometimes billed as Jackson Hole's first trophy home.

Underhyped attractions in Jackson include the **River Runners' Museum** (1255 S. U.S. 89/191/26; 800/458–7238 or 307/733–6203), part of Mad River Outfitters' architecturally intriguing headquarters on the south end of town. Inside a

★ Stick 'Em Up ★

In summer, tourists crowd the Town Square Monday through Saturday evenings to watch a costumed cast salute Jackson's proud history of vigilantism with an elaborate reenacted shootout.

BULL MARKET

While gazing at the elk-antler arches in Town Square, the occasional aghast Jackson visitor asks, "How many elk did they have to kill to get all those antlers?" In fact, none. Elk shed their antlers naturally ever year in the late winter. By April the antlers litter the ground at the National Elk Refuge like giant, pointy twigs. That's when the Boy Scouts sweep through, per a 1957 agreement with the U.S. Fish & Wildlife Service. They gather, bundle, and weigh some 10,000 pounds of antlers each year.

The fruits of the Scouts' labor go on display annually the weekend before Memorial Day, lining the walkways and stacked six feet high on pallets in Town Square. The bundles are auctioned off as part of Jackson's lively **Elkfest,** during which artists and other antler aficionados place bids while the other townsfolk chow on picnic food, take in outdoor concerts, and resist the temptation to make "nice rack" jokes.

Bundles of elk antlers line Jackson's streets during the annual Elkfest celebration.

giant right-angle triangle with a reflective facade, this small museum pairs some of the improbable early dinghies and rafts used to tackle white water with photo collections selling the romantic life of the river guide.

Another sight more puzzled at than promoted is the **ArtSPOT,** a frequently updated public canvas that used to be a gas-station sign. You'll find the multimedia mural, created by local artists, on the corner of Broadway and Scott Lane on the west side of town.

SKI RESORTS

Jackson Hole Mountain Resort (general info 888/333–7766; snow conditions 307/733–2291) entices globe-trotting powderhounds with two steep mountains, some 450 inches of snow per year, and awesome backcountry runs. There's a **Nordic Center** (307/739–2629) too, combining more than 10 miles of groomed track with close-up Teton views. Headquarters is the chi-chi hospitality circus of **Teton Village,** a bustling cluster of Swiss chalets along Moose–Wilson Road that specializes in all things *après.*

The ★**JACKSON HOLE AERIAL TRAM** (888/333–7766; Village Dr.) sails the void between "the Vill" and the 10,450-foot summit of **Rendezvous Mountain,** the largest vertical rise for a lift in North America. The Hole's iconic "big red box" got a little bigger and a little redder in 2006, when the original 1960s tram was retired in favor of an upgrade. The new tram hauls up to a hundred skiers, hikers, and sightseers on a nine-minute ride through the very thin Teton air. The whir of the cable is often the only sound while awed passengers drink in mountain views usually reserved for the eagles. Tram-only tickets are available at the ticket center next to the terminal. The cozier **Bridger Gondola** (behind the Bridger Center) "only" takes you to 9,095 feet, but it's free on winter evenings, and it drops you off at a sexy contemporary bistro (*see* Couloir, *below*).

In summer the tram and the gondola offer equally astounding views, plus sweat-free trail access for hikers and backpackers hitting the high country. Mountain bikers swarm over miles of single-track in the warm months (with a quad lift to boot), and if you've ever wanted to hurl your child into the air with a giant slingshot, you can do that on the **bungee trampoline.** Get the full menu of summer activities from the **Mountain Sports School** (Bridger Center; 307/739–2779). **Jackson Hole Sports** (Bridger Center; 307/739–2687) rents ski gear in the winter and bikes in the summer, in addition to selling everything from Frisbee golf disks and performance wear to Jackson Hole coffee

The Jackson Hole Aerial Tram zooms up more than 4,100 feet in roughly nine minutes.

A powderhound hits the Jackson
Hole Mountain Resort ski runs.

Teton Village Ski Resort.

PEOPLE IN THE PARKS:
SHANE MOORE, WILDLIFE FILMMAKER

A lifelong Jacksonian and an accomplished cinematographer, Shane Moore has been making films in Greater Yellowstone for more than 25 years. Among his credits is the already classic *Christmas in Yellowstone,* produced for PBS's *Nature.*

Brian Kevin: How have you seen Jackson change over the years?

Shane Moore: When I grew up here, Jackson was just transitioning from a ranching/tourist community into very much a resort community, but there's been a lot of good with that. The wildlife around here keeps getting better and better—it turns out people are actually using the backcountry less than they did twenty years ago. The real wonderful opportunities for solitude are still there. And it's a very interesting and vibrant and lively community.

BK: So what do the experts know about wildlife-watching that the rest of us don't?

SM: It's the little, subtle things that lead to the wonderful events we occasionally get to film. For a lot of people, the experience is quite rushed. You can never experience all of the park in one trip anyway, so don't even try is my advice. Take a little slice and get in tune to it. You start to learn little things about a place—who's doing what? What coyote tends to

be stealing fish from the otters? Then by watching that coyote, I know where to find the otters, even if they've been in the den for hours.

BK: When you have folks in town who want to experience the parks, where do you take them?

SM: With youngsters especially, I think it's really important to interact with nature, so fishing is a wonderful experience. You know, if it becomes too much of a boardwalk experience, there's something that's lost. So I really encourage people to just get off the road and listen to a place, feel it, and smell it. Those are the things that television never does, and there's no substitute.

BK: Is there a sense in which it feels less "wild" to film in a national park, where there are buildings and roads, than in, say, Alaska?

SM: For some people, seeing something in Yellowstone from the road seems to diminish the experience. I think that view is completely wrong. It's a very authentic experience, and I don't think there's any place in the world where you can see the equivalent of the types of things that you can see in Yellowstone these days from the road.

mugs. You can also get the logo gear without even visiting the hill in downtown Jackson at the **Jackson Hole Resort Store** (50 N. Center St.; 307/739–2767).

While JHMR tends to get all the glory and most of the out-of-town visitors, **Snow King Resort** (400 E. Snow King Ave.; 800/522–5464 or 307/733–5200), Jackson's "other" hill, swarms with in-the-know townies on powder days. You won't find a lot of beginners' runs on this über-steep "racer's" mountain, but you can take a lesson with a legend. The ski school is run by one Bill Briggs, who made first ski descents on all three Tetons, including the Grand in 1971.

The crowd on the slopes tends to be a thriftier, down-to-earth bunch of diehards, prone to take advantage of the hill's two-hour morning lift tickets and make a few after-dark runs. Visible from almost anywhere else in Jackson, the illuminated hill glows like a big, white beacon on winter nights. In the summer, a wide plastic track winds 2,500 feet down Snow King mountain, a thrilling **alpine slide** you navigate on a tiny vehicle that's part go-kart, part toboggan. The velocity can be intense, but more cautious sliders can brake to admire views of town and wildflower meadows on the way down.

Crossing Teton Pass to reach **Grand Targhee Resort** (3300 E. Ski Hill Rd., Alta; 800/827–4433 or 307/353–2300), you abandon the glitz of Jackson altogether, swapping resort-town ambience for piles upon piles of the white stuff. Targhee remains small and relatively unspoiled, a family-style resort that benefits from a geographical and meteorological quirk. On the west side of the Teton Range about an hour's drive from Jackson, Targhee is in the path of storms moving west across Idaho and Wyoming. When these pressure systems hit the wall-like ridge of the mountains, they tend to hover, depositing some 50 feet of snow in a good year.

(above) Snow-mobiling through fresh powder at Togwotee Pass; (bottom) a freestyle stunt at the Jackson Hole Mountain Festival.

The breadth of wide-open runs at Targhee favors intermediate skiers. There are two small terrain parks, and the pristine nearby backcountry has enticed the likes of the extreme athletes and filmmakers from Teton Gravity Research. Targhee's shred cred has increased significantly in recent years, and expanded lodging, dining, and shopping are on the way, so hit the slopes now while the hill is still a local secret.

OTHER WINTER ACTIVITIES

Love them or hate them, snowmobiles are a popular and efficient way to explore the vast network of national forest trails surrounding Jackson. Outfitters like **Jackson Hole Snowmobile Tours** (515 N. Cache St.;

800/633–1733 or 307/733–6850) can rent sleds or lead trips along some of the more popular routes. The **Togwotee Pass** area (off U.S. 26/287, 20 mi east of Grand Teton National Park) is holy ground for sledders, 70 miles of groomed trails like white, forested corridors through the Absarokas.

If you prefer snowmobiling as a spectator sport, consider the annual **World Championship Snowmobile Hill Climb** at Snow King Resort, where thousands gather to see a horde of snowmobilers—some of them sober—try to ascend a 1,300-foot, nearly vertical slope. It's a winter spectacle of Darwinian proportions.

Jackson Hole Iditarod Sled Dog Tours (800/554–7388 or 307/733–7388) is run by multiple-Iditarod veteran Frank Teasley. On a half-day trip an eager team of huskies pants as they pull you through Granite Creek Canyon south of town. The cold wind loses its sting when you know the trail leads to a dip in a quiet natural hot spring.

Summer Activities

On the west side of the Elk Refuge, the Flat Creek drainage near the **Jackson National Fish Hatchery** (1500 Fish Hatchery Rd.; 307/733–2510) is near-sacred ground for local anglers, a busy fly-only river with copious hatches throughout the late summer and fall. The experts come out to stalk the creek's notoriously wily cutthroat, while first-time anglers head up the road to the fishery's stocked, half-acre **Sleeping Indian Pond,** a popular place to fish with kids.

The Snake River roars to life south of Jackson, earning its reputation for classic white water in an eight-mile stretch known as the Grand Canyon of the Snake River. **Snake River Kayak & Canoe** (365 N. Cache St.; 307/733–9999) can lead you down in bobbing raft-kayak hybrids called "duckies." **Mad River Boat Trips** (1255 S. U.S. 89/191/26; 800/458–7238) uses rafts and feeds you a top-notch picnic meal to boot. If you can tear your eyes from the rocks and waves, watch for osprey and bald eagles in the surrounding firs and pines.

Hang gliding and paragliding are enormously popular around Jackson. The abrupt nature of the Tetons' east face allows aerialists to launch from breathtaking heights and watch the green-and-blue floor of Jackson Hole tumble away below. **Jackson Hole Paragliding** (307/690–8726) and **Cowboy Up Hang Gliding** (307/413–4164) both offer lessons and tandem flights. **Wyoming Balloon Company** (307/739–0900) can take you into the sky with even less effort on your part, and they do it beneath a huge nylon envelope with a psychedelic wildlife scene on it.

Canoeing in the shadow of Mount Moran.

Within galloping distance of Jackson are more than a dozen ranches and lodges offering horseback rides. The visitor center in town can help you find the right one for your party and skill level. **Mill Iron Ranch** (3495 E. Horse Creek Rd.; 888/808–6390 or 307/733–6390) stands out for its scenery. This fourth-generation ranch 10 miles south of town is surrounded by rolling green hills and almost hoodoo-like rock formations.

THE ARTS

A cluster of modern, angular buildings makes up the **Jackson Hole Center for the Arts** campus (240 S. Glenwood St.; general info 307/734–8956, box office 307/733–4900). Four art galleries cultivate a vibe of experimentation, so you're as likely to see found-object trash sculpture as you are alpine photography. There's also a 500-seat theater that has pretty eclectic programming. On my last visit, for instance, the schedule included the Jackson Hole Symphony Orchestra, jazz saxophonist Branford Marsalis, and the squeaky-voiced comedian Gilbert Gottfried.

In summer and fall, the center is a popular starting point for the city's Thursday night open-studio **ARTwalks,** especially since the best contemporary galleries are found in the surrounding "SoBo" (south of Broadway) neighborhood. **Muse Gallery** (62 S. Glenwood St.; 307/733–0555) and **Lyndsay McCandless Contemporary** (130 S. Jackson St.; 307/734–0649) tend to display the sort of avant-garde apples that fall farthest from Jackson's landscapes-and-wildlife-art tree.

From rows of dangling spurs to some of Jackson's creepiest taxidermy, anything with a bit of cowboy cachet gets nailed to the wall of the Million Dollar Cowboy Bar.

NIGHTLIFE

The **Million Dollar Cowboy Bar** (25 N. Cache Dr.; 307/733–2207) is an Old West saloon gone self-aware. The landmark bar with the garish neon cowboy sign predates Prohibition, and they've evidently never thrown anything out. From rows of dangling spurs to some of Jackson's creepiest taxidermy, anything with a bit of cowboy cachet gets nailed to the wall here. The unabashedly kitschy room reverberates with live music six nights a week in summer (both kinds, country and western), and the dance floor is packed wall-to-wall on weekends with both locals and tourists.

There's a giant stuffed moose dangling over the dance floor at the **Mangy Moose** (Teton Village; 307/733–4913), but it has never stopped sweaty hordes from packing in before the small wooden stage. The concert calendar at the Moose is always a litany of top-notch touring bands, oscillating freely between hip-hop, blues, jam-band, and bluegrass acts. The crowd is young and the microbrews are local inside the pine-beamed pub. The party sometimes spills out onto a large outdoor deck.

WHERE TO EAT

Couloir. Lunch or dinner at Couloir begins with a complimentary ride on the Bridger Gondola from Teton Village to the restaurant's 9,095-foot perch. In summer you'll want to sprint to the patio, where large glass panes offer a sweeping view of the valley. (But if it's too cold to eat outdoors, don't fret; the dining room has floor-to-ceiling windows.) Handsomely plated sandwiches, pasta, and seafood make for an elegant lunch on the slopes, but it's the prix-fixe dinner menus and vast wine and cocktail lists that make Couloir stand out. Organic produce, fish, and game all get innovative treatment—think cornmeal-dusted oysters and wild-boar gnocchi. *On Rendezvous Mountain; 307/739–2675.* **$$$$**

Snake River Grill. For many years after it opened in 1993, Snake River Grill was *the* place in Jackson for contemporary white-tablecloth dining. Today it feels a bit like a heritage supper club. Though comfy, the "rustic-luxe" ambience of leather booths, stone fireplaces, and lodgepole beams isn't as novel as it once was, and the crowd can be pretty sedate. The menu, however, remains cutting-edge and well executed. Entrées like pumpkin seed–crusted salmon and melt-in-your-mouth bison pot roast are paired with a wine list that's consistently recognized as one of the region's best. *84 E. Broadway Ave.; 307/733–0557.* **$$$$**

Bar J Chuckwagon. It's more of a dinner theater than actual restaurant, but the Bar J is something of an institution in the Hole. Tucked away off the Moose–Wilson Road south of Teton Village, the Chuckwagon is a bastion of old timey Cowboy West—or at least the Gene-Autrified movie version. A talented in-house cowboy band serenades a 700-person indoor dining room as

★ *Special Souvenir* ★

At Jedediah's House of Sourdough, you can buy sourdough starter that comes from a mother sponge reportedly older than Jackson itself. Truly a taste of pioneer life!

guests slog through heaping plates of barbecued meats and cowboy fixings. Vegetarians might want to pack a bag of carrot sticks or just come to enjoy the music. *4200 W. Bar J Chuckwagon Rd., Wilson; 307/733–3370.* **$$$–$$$$**

★TRIO. Local foodies and out-of-towners tired of lodge decor make up the smartly dressed crowd at this chef-driven bistro. The room's modern, minimalist feel benefits from an open floor plan, an exposed kitchen, and a sexy marble bar. The seasonal entrées rely heavily on fish and game, such as elk Bolognese or trout amandine. A side dish of waffle fries with blue-cheese fondue is as luscious as anything on the dessert menu. This isn't really a spot for kids, but the wood-fired pizzas might work for their palates and your wallet. *45 S. Glenwood Dr.; 307/734–8038.* **$$–$$$$**

Thai Me Up. Locals crowd this downtown lunch and dinner joint that's half contemporary bistro and half kitschy-authentic Thai dining room, complete with small winking Buddhas. The menu spins the same sort of fusion, with knockout Thai curries and noodle dishes using a few distinctly non-Asian ingredients like tomatillos or rainbow trout. Vegetarians and vegans are welcome here like no place else in town. Try a Thai Russian (White Russian with coconut milk) at the tiny, funky bar. *75 E. Pearl St.; 307/733–0005.* **$$–$$$**

Snake River Brewing Company. The emphasis at Jackson's signature brewery is rightly on beer; the food is tailored to the suds. The brewpub's high-ceilinged room smells pleasantly of hops and yeast. The menu is loaded with sandwiches, pastas, and wood-fired pizzas, plus a couple of standouts like the veal brat with spicy beer mustard. Happy hour from 4 to 6 PM is taken seriously by many locals, but the place can become abruptly festive at all hours of the day. A hefty roster of seasonal beers complements SRB's classic pale ale and rich Zonker stout. A self-guided brewery tour allows for a glimpse behind the scene. *265 S. Millward St.; 307/739–2337.* **$$**

Mountain High Pizza Pie. Many a Teton backpacker has fantasized about one of Mountain High's monster pesto-veggie calzones while choking down another freeze-dried meal on the trail. This humble hut downtown caters to families, hungry hikers, and anyone on a budget with pizzas, calzones, subs, and suds. Nothing too exotic here, but wheat and deep-dish crusts make this a better choice than the chains. In summer the picnic tables on the patio get slammed. Mountain High also delivers if you don't feel like braving the crowds. *120 W. Broadway Ave.; 307/733–3646.* **$–$$**

See the West Yellowstone map.

★JEDEDIAH'S HOUSE OF SOURDOUGH. On summer mornings you might spot a line out the door of this historic Jackson breakfast institution. Once you're inside, though, a warm, slightly vinagery scent floats in from the kitchen, and you'll forget the wait as you tuck in to a stack of blueberry sourdough pancakes ("sourjacks"). The best tables are on the shaded, breezy deck. Lunch sandwiches on sourdough bread include a thick buffalo burger, and kids can choose from a couple of smaller plates at both meals. (They don't serve dinner.) The sourdough starter for sale at the counter comes from a mother sponge older than Jackson itself. *135 E. Broadway Ave.; 307/733–5671. $–$$*

WEST YELLOWSTONE

See the West Yellowstone map.

It was tourism that spawned this little town at the end of the Union Pacific rail line in 1908, and it's tourism that sustains it today. In summer the strip in "West" is a lively faux-Western promenade of souvenir stands, fly shops, hotels, and cafés. In winter the high bumblebee whine of snowmobiles is omnipresent, and the machines seem to outnumber cars on city streets two to one. That said, the town is idyllically set at the foot of the skyscraping Madison Range, just south of the point where the Gallatin River cuts dramatically through the cliffs of Gallatin Canyon. If you do manage to find some locals, they're likely to be laid-back folks with a passion for the outdoors.

EXPLORING AROUND TOWN

There is something weirdly postmodern about visiting Yellowstone as a tourist and, while there, going to a museum dedicated to the history of tourism in Yellowstone. It's still worth a visit, though, to the **Yellowstone Historic Center** (104 Yellowstone Ave.; 406/646–1100), where weathered iron railroad equipment, several generations of yellowed photographs, and early visitors' journals document the human experience in the park. The collection fills the restored 1909 Union Pacific train depot, a great stone-columned building with a short, symbolic stretch of rail behind. When the drafty depot closes its doors in the fall, a condensed **winter gallery** (222 Yellowstone Ave.; 406/646–7461) displays artifacts just up the road.

Observing the "product-testing" of new bear-proof storage technologies at the Grizzly & Wolf Discovery Center is a voyeuristic thrill, particularly since the determined grizzlies usually emerge triumphant.

The nonprofit **Grizzly & Wolf Discovery Center** (201 South Canyon Rd.; 800/257–2570) is a well-managed education and research facility that takes in animals otherwise likely to be euthanized. The center is a good stop for young children who lack the patience for wildlife-watching in the park. In summer naturalists lead programs twice daily, during which kids learn about bears' scavenging habits by hiding food and watching the bears seek it out. Observing the "product-testing" of new bear-proof storage technologies is another voyeuristic thrill, particularly since the determined grizzlies usually emerge triumphant, leaving twisted metal and plastic shards in their wake.

Twenty-seven miles northwest of town, the **Earthquake Lake Visitor Center** (U.S. 287; 406/682–7620) sits atop the 80 million tons of rock that slid into the Madison River during the 1959 Hebgen

Lake Earthquake (*see below*). Interpretive displays and a 15-minute movie retell the story of the night the earth bucked. A short walking trail leads to vistas of the scarred Sheep Mountain and Quake Lake itself, a six-mile lake that used to be a green river valley dotted with campsites and cabins. Among the haunting sites at Quake Lake is the **ghost village,** visible from a dirt road that turns south five miles east of the visitor center. There, on the far side of the river, a scatter of decrepit wooden cabins looks eerily untouched, each one tilting drunkenly in the position left to it by receding floodwaters.

OTHER ACTIVITIES

A few miles northeast of town, **Hebgen Lake** sloshes in the shadow of the Madisons, a 12,500-acre playground for fisherman and boaters behind the man-made Hebgen Lake Dam. You can put in on the south side of the lake at **Lonesomehurst Campground** (on Hebgen Lake Rd., 8 mi west of West Yellowstone off U.S. 20) or on the east side at **Rainbow Point Campground** (on Rainbow Point Rd., 5 mi north of West Yellowstone off U.S. 191), and several resort marinas offer rentals. The often choppy waters yield a healthy supply of brown and rainbow trout. Ice shanties belonging to truly dedicated fisherman pepper the lake's north end during the winter.

THE HEBGEN LAKE EARTHQUAKE

It prompted evacuations at Old Faithful, caused rock slides in California, and dropped water tables as far away as Puerto Rico. The magnitude 7.5 earthquake that struck on August 17, 1959, was the strongest and deadliest in Montana's history. Though the shaking lasted less than a minute, the Sheep Mountain landslide poured into the Madison River Canyon at 100 miles per hour, destroying a campground and a mile-long stretch of highway and sending 30-foot waves in both directions. In Yellowstone, some 160 geysers broke into a chorus of simultaneous eruption, and many were permanently altered.

Twenty-eight people were killed by falling rocks or drowned as the river rapidly pooled behind the debris to form Quake Lake. Fearing a flood, the U.S. Army Corps of Engineers worked around the clock for weeks to dig a slough through the debris. Fault scarps from the quake reach 21 feet high, and the implausible walls of dirt can be explored in spots like the **Cabin Creek Scarp Area** (off U.S. 287, 4 mi west of Earthquake Lake Visitor Center).

North of West Yellowstone, the gray walls of Gallatin Canyon close in around the Gallatin River, transforming it into a frothy, roaring white-water mecca. The Shoshone called this river "Cut-tuh-o-gwa" or "swift water." Local paddlers call its toughest section "the Mad Mile," a stretch of continuous white water north of Big Sky that drenches bold rafters and kayakers as they navigate rapids with names like "Screaming Left Turn" and "Rodeo Hole." An hour north of town at Gallatin Gateway, **Montana Whitewater** (63960 Gallatin Rd.,

406/763–4465) leads full- and half-day rafting trips that are likely to soak you. They run mellower stretches too, in case you'd rather not, you know, wet yourself.

The tiny **Bear's Den Cinema** (15 N. Electric St.; 406/646–7777) shows first-run movies throughout the year, but if you're going to catch a flick in Yellowstone, wouldn't you rather see one that's six stories tall? In the summer the **Yellowstone IMAX Theatre** (101 S. Canyon St.; 406/646–4100) runs the 30-minute park documentary *Yellowstone* repeatedly between 9 AM and 9 PM. The film is a decent intro to the park, with some memorable historical quotes and cute bear hijinks. The theater mixes it up with a few other nature-themed IMAX films during snowmobile season.

NIGHTLIFE

Generally speaking, you'll find more excitement stargazing on a Saturday night in West Yellowstone than you will in any of the town's no-frills bars and pubs. The Stagecoach Inn's **Coachman Lounge** (406/646–7381) keeps busy on weekends, though, with live rock music loud enough to make your teeth rattle. The bar draws a lively crowd of snowmobilers and other winter adventurers when the powder flies, possibly on account of the big fireplace but more likely for the strong drinks. This being Montana, you'll also find the ubiquitous video gambling machines.

WHERE TO EAT

Sydney's Mountain Bistro. Tiny, ten-table Sydney's could hold its own in a much larger city on the strength of its kitchen and stylish food presentation. The short menu hypes local and fresh ingredients in surprisingly sophisticated dishes like luscious squash ravioli and cilantro-lime Thai calamari. The room itself is pretty guileless, cozy with simple wood trim and some art deco posters on the walls, but no other menu in West Yellowstone aims this high. *38 Canyon St.; 406/646–7660.* **$$$–$$$$**

Mocha Mamma's. It's not a meal exactly, but the best espresso in West Yellowstone comes from this tiny, five-stool coffee bar tucked into the corner of the outdoor apparel store Freeheel & Wheel. The espresso is locally roasted, and the baristas get it right every time. The bar's big selling point is the young staff, an active and enthusiastic crew that can relate as much about local skiing and mountain biking as any guide in town, all over a blueberry bagel and a cup of joe. *40 Yellowstone Ave.; 406/646–7744.* **$**

CODY *See the Downtown Cody map.*

The tourism industry in Cody has done more to preserve the rugged myth of the cowboy than country music and truck commercials combined. At once more authentically Western than other Yellowstone gateway towns (it's the "Rodeo Capital of the World") and more pedestrian (it has a Wal-Mart), Cody is in large part what you make of it. "Buffalo Bill" Cody knew this when he and a group of developers essentially willed the town into existence in the 1890s. Cody personally courted settlers, brought the railroad to town, and convinced President Roosevelt to dam the Shoshone River to provide power.

Today the Shoshone flows through a town filled with century-old structures, Old West museums, Western-furniture galleries, and one giant rodeo arena. Though it's an hour's drive along the Buffalo Bill Scenic Byway to reach Yellowstone's east entrance, the river vistas and rock formations along the way make it one of the most scenic routes into the park.

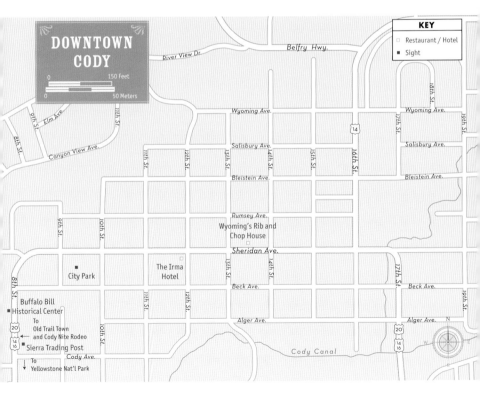

Ready, aim, fire: art and guns share top billing at Cody's Buffalo Bill Historical Center.

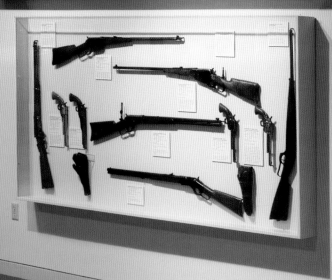

Exploring Around Town

The **Buffalo Bill Historical Center** (720 Sheridan Ave.; 307/587–4771) is Cody's answer to the Smithsonian, five themed museums in one seven-acre facility, each as elaborate as the Wild West shows promoted by the center's namesake. The **Whitney Gallery of Western Art** includes stunning early paintings and photos of Yellowstone by Thomas Moran and William Henry Jackson, plus a gallery of splashy contemporary work. Three other museums focus on Plains Indian art, Yellowstone natural history, and old Buffalo Bill himself. The **Cody Firearms Museum** is by a long shot the least conventional, a maze of glass cases so full of antique pistols and rifles it would have made even Charlton Heston a little nervous.

A bright red-and-green trolley rolls up to the historical center three times a day during summer to load passengers for the **Cody Trolley Tours** (kiosk at the Irma Hotel, 1192 Sheridan Ave.; 307/527–7043). An ebullient tour guide dressed as sharpshooter Annie Oakley narrates a one-hour trip aboard the air-conditioned car, dropping tidbits of local history along with a few well-timed groaners. The trip includes a visit to **Old Trail Town** (1831 DeMaris Dr., 866/868–2111), an atmospheric street of log cabins, clapboard stables, and swinging-door storefronts. The architectural relics were collected from across western Wyoming and reassembled museum-style on the original Cody townsite. The trolley also heads west through the striped sedimentary cliffs of Shoshone Canyon—literally through them, via a series of arching tunnels—to visit the **Buffalo Bill Dam and Reservoir.** At 325 feet tall, the dam was once the world's largest, and it remains impressive for its unlikely positioning, wedged tightly between the sheer walls of a plummeting granite canyon.

Cheers echo off the roof of the grandstand as another bronc and dusty rider burst from the chute at the ★CODY NITE RODEO (on the west edge of town on U.S. 14/16/20; 800/207–0744). Every night in June, July, and August, you'll find amateur and pro cowpeople clinging to jerking broncos, wrestling 300-pound steers to the ground, and casting lassos at sprinting calves. If you've never experienced a rodeo, there is really no better place to do it, with the high, brown Wyoming desert as a backdrop, the pungent smell of stock in the air, and more dudes in chaps than at a Harley Davidson rally. Aside from some ribald humor from the announcers' booth, the events are kid-friendly. Young rodeo fans are invited into the arena

Cody

Yellowstone National Park

(opposite top) Bonanza meets the baroque at the Buffalo Bill Historical Center; (bottom) the stagecoach used in Buffalo Bill's Wild West Show.

There's nothing ironic about this cowboy finery— in Cody, it's a lifestyle.

before each show for a "calf scramble," where packs of screaming children terrorize a baby cow by trying to pluck a ribbon off of it. The week of July 4th, the big-purse **Cody Stampede Rodeo** attracts the world's best riders and a Stetson-clad crowd of diehard fans.

Other Activities

Between Cody and Yellowstone, some dozen guest ranches tuck in among the river vistas and rock formations of the **Buffalo Bill Scenic Byway,** and they all have stables. Most offer a slate of horseback trips ranging from afternoon trots to weeklong wilderness trips in the surrounding Shoshone National Forest. **Bill Cody Ranch** (2604 Yellowstone Hwy.; 307/587–2097) is among those offering day rides for nonguests, including beginners. Twenty-five miles east of town, they lead afternoon trips that top out above 7,000 feet, with limitless Absaroka views and trail-prepared cowboy lunches.

If you need to pick up any last-minute gear for your exploits in the parks, hit the **Sierra Trading Post Outlet Store** (1402 8th St.; 307/578–5802), a crucial and budget-friendly adventure headquarters.

Nightlife

On Friday nights in July and August, a forest of lawn chairs sprouts in front of the park bandshell for **summer concerts at City Park** (908 Sheridan Ave.; 307/587–2777). The acts are mostly local, ranging from jazz combos to—surprise!—cowboy balladeers. The 6 PM curtain time, along with the park's playground and mini-golf course, make this a popular night out for families with younger children.

When Cody locals feel like kicking their spurs in the air and waving them like they just don't care, they head to **Cassie's Supper Club & Dance Hall** (214 Yellowstone Ave.; 307/527–5500), which the proprietors will tell you has been entertaining Cody-ites since 1922. Until the 1930s it was entertaining them with prostitutes, and artifacts from this era of ill repute decorate the massive wooden dining, drinking, and dancing space, including a robe worn by the bar's namesake madam. The atmosphere is twangy roadhouse, with live country music most nights in summer.

Where to Eat

The Irma. Although he probably didn't have anything to do with the 1950s-diner-style sign outside, Buffalo Bill Cody himself built the showy Irma Hotel and Restaurant in 1902. In one of the restaurant's two dining rooms stretches an ornate cherrywood backbar presented

BUFFALO BILL WRANGLING

To pay your respects to the impresario of the Wild West, you may have to look outside of his namesake town. Buffalo Bill Cody died after falling on hard times. A bad debt to a pair of shyster promoters in Denver kept him performing in circuses almost into his 70s. He died there in 1917, and folks back in Wyoming blanched when Mrs. Cody proclaimed that Bill, in a last-minute change of heart, decided to be buried in Colorado rather than at his presumed gravesite in Cody. Controversy still rages as to whether the same Denver shysters bribed or harassed Cody's wife into the arrangement.

He was buried on Lookout Mountain near present-day Golden, Colorado, and a niece declared afterwards that she would "fight every person in Colorado" to bring him "back" to Cody. The Cody American Legion felt similarly. They posted a $100,000 reward in 1948 for anyone who could steal and "return" the body. In response, Denver's Legion put up guards until the city could deepen the grave and cover it with thirty tons of concrete. Today, though, rumors persist that some Cody-ite pulled it off, that Buffalo Bill lies in an unmarked grave somewhere in Shoshone country.

Cody's Buffalo Bill Historical Center.

to Cody by Queen Victoria in 1900. The antique cash register and archival photos on the wall also contribute to the room's museum feel. The menu is eclectic, ranging from omelets to Mexican entrées and an occasional wild card like whiskey bread pudding. Children under six eat free from the breakfast and lunch buffets. *1192 Sheridan Ave.; 307/587–4221.* **$$–$$$**

Wyoming's Rib & Chop House. So you spent the evening watching people in chaps ride and wrestle giant steers, and now you want to eat one. This Montana and Wyoming chain has a reputation for turning out some of the region's best red meat, like the tender, hand-cut rib eye. Tangy, slow-cooked baby back ribs are another carnivore favorite. The smallish dining room in this squat, brick building fills quickly in summer, so reservations are a must. Grab a table near the giant front windows for excellent people-watching. *1367 Sheridan Ave.; 307/527–7731.* **$–$$$**

⊙ GARDINER

Yellowstone's first "gateway town" may have been created as a form of revenge. Its founder, James McCartney, has the dubious distinction of having been one of the park's first profiteers. He and a partner informally claimed land and set up a shabby hotel at Mammoth Hot Springs in 1871. When the Feds finally gave an angry McCartney the boot in 1879, he went out and founded Gardiner, right up against the park's northern boundary. Now the community is Yellowstone's only year-round entry point.

Gardiner boomed with the arrival of the Northern Pacific in 1902, and by the time the railroad shuttered almost 50 years later, it was a well-established tourism hotspot. The town is still a micro-mecca for lodging and other visitor facilities, but it comes off as a quieter, more genuine place than other entrance communities. The Yellowstone River flows right through, augmented south of town by the Gardner. Note the different spelling between the river and the town—both are named for mountain man Johnson Gardner, but the village adopted a phonetic rendering based on renowned trapper and storyteller Jim Bridger's southern accent.

EXPLORING AROUND TOWN

The regal **Roosevelt Arch** (park entrance on North Entrance Rd.) was built to wow the early waves of Yellowstone visitors, who were nonplussed by the landscape around the park's north entrance. As the park's chief engineer, Hiram Chittenden, noted sourly in one annual report, "The first impression of visitors entering the park was very unfavorable." President Theodore Roosevelt himself laid the cornerstone for the arch in 1903. At 50 feet high, the basalt structure goes a long way toward compensating for dull scenery. It even partially makes up for the kitschy tourist strip that's since developed along Gardiner's share of the park entrance road.

The **Yellowstone National Park Heritage & Research Center** (200 Old Yellowstone Trail; 307/344–2664), while not exactly a tourist attraction, is an astounding depository of all things Yellowstone, from crates of historical documents to early staff uniforms to preserved plant specimens. Parts of the research library are open to the public, and there's a small history exhibit in the lobby, but the best way to glimpse the recesses is to join one of the biweekly summer tours, open to a mere ten visitors at a time. This will give you a truly unique glimpse at a low-key Yellowstone treasure.

Where to Eat

Sawtooth Deli. Gardiner is not an epicure's town, but inside this humble-looking storefront are some killer huevos and very respectable New York–style deli sandwiches. If you nab one of two tiny outdoor tables, you can attack your pastrami on rye with a fine view of the Roosevelt Arch, and you might find yourself seated next to a Yellowstone maven from the nearby Heritage & Research Center. Dinner options include wood-fired pizza, pasta, and local trout. *220 W. Park St.; 406/848–7600.* **$$**

Where to Stay

The stars look incredibly bright and close out here.

Fireworks over Teton Village during the Jackson Hole Mountain Festival.

Whether you're stepping out of your room into the pine-pillared lobby of a historic park hotel or nestling deeper into your sleeping bag while gray jays whistle at the dawn, waking up inside a national park is a singular experience. Lodging in the gateway communities can be equally adventuresome, as the parks' peripheries attract a funky collection of sexy resorts, quilt-and-teacup B&Bs, and offbeat roadhouse motels.

Park lodging terminology can be a little tricky. It's useful to remember that, more often than not, a "lodge" in Yellowstone and Grand Teton refers to a campus made up of cabins, cottages, and one or more "main lodge" buildings with dining rooms, lounges, and other public spaces. Public spaces in all of the park accommodations are open to nonguests for sightseeing or hanging out.

ARE YOU IN OR ARE YOU OUT?

Your biggest choice is whether to stay inside or outside the park. Park lodging tends to be a little pricier than a night's stay in the gateway towns, but many visitors find the cost is offset by the obvious perks of scenery and proximity to park attractions. Then you have to weigh the intangibles. Cabins, inns, and hotels inside Yellowstone and Grand

Teton usually date back a few decades or more. If you're after a historic vibe, then you're likely also signing on for a smaller room and a more casual attitude toward upkeep than you'd find outside the park. You won't find in-room televisions inside Yellowstone, and they're rare in Grand Teton. Coffeemakers, telephones, and private bathrooms aren't always a given; neither are heat or air-conditioning. The best rule of thumb for booking a room inside the parks is not to take anything for granted. If a particular amenity is important to you, ask about it upon reservation. (*See* the Practical Information chapter for more information about phone and Internet access in and near the parks.)

Maintaining cabins and hotel rooms in Yellowstone and Grand Teton is a constant battle for park concessionaires, and creaky hinges, leaky faucets, or torn or missing window screens are not at all unusual. Concessionaire staff members are helpful and sympathetic, though, and they'll deal swiftly with serious problems.

GET A ROOM

June through August is peak season in Greater Yellowstone, when rooms fill fast and prices are at their highest. It's wise to make reservations a year or more in advance for the more sought-after park accommodations (Old Faithful Inn, Lake Hotel, and Jenny Lake Lodge). You can get away with six months' advance reservation for most cabins, and even less if you're not picky about location or amenities. The reservation timeline varies greatly outside the park. Generally speaking, the more unusual your chosen accommodation, the earlier you ought to book. Chains have more last-minute options.

You can often save money on lodging by visiting in the "bumper seasons" of April and May or September and October. Winter deals are most prevalent in January, when extreme temperatures put a damper on tourism.

In the listings below, frequently repeated phone numbers and Web sites are due to the fact that **Xanterra Parks & Resorts** manages all lodging in Yellowstone, and **Grand Teton Lodge Company** manages most properties in Grand Teton. These concessionaires and others also manage many of the campgrounds, though some are administered by the NPS. This divvied-up arrangement means that there's no single clearinghouse for campground information. Outside the park, **Jackson Hole Central Reservations** (888/838–6606; www.jacksonholewy.com) and **West Yellowstone Central Reservations**

The Old Faithful Inn is one of the crown jewels of the national park system.

(888/646–7077; www.yellowstonereservation.com) are useful for "one-stop shopping."

 # LODGES, HOTELS, AND INNS

YELLOWSTONE'S LOWER LOOP

OLD FAITHFUL

Old Faithful Snow Lodge. Clean and contemporary, the Snow Lodge is the newest lodging option in the park, completed in 1999. While the timber and wrought-iron interior can't compare to that of the neighboring Old Faithful Inn, its fireplace lobby and plush, airy sitting room are still ideal for lounging. The guest rooms are standard modern, each with a full bathroom and wildlife-themed bedspreads. True to its name, the Snow Lodge is one of just two in-park hotels open in winter, accessible by snowcoach or snowmobile. *Old Faithful; 307/344–7311 or 866/439–7375; www.travelyellowstone.com.* **$$$$**

★**OLD FAITHFUL INN.** The steep and many-gabled roof of the Old Faithful Inn cuts a regal profile across the Yellowstone sky, flags waving from its widow's walk. Once inside the iron-studded front doors, you're engulfed by the seven-story space. The inn's awesome main hall has a 90-foot ceiling, a gargantuan stone fireplace, and a spiraling series of intricately hand-wrought wooden balconies. Known as the Old House, this portion was completed in 1903, and is one of the most photographed destinations in the park. Room choices vary from wood-framed quarters with claw-foot tubs to more modern units in the east and west additions. Those with the best geyser basin views are in the Old House and the west wing. For a view that only a handful of park visitors ever see, ask a bellman to put you on the list to follow Inn staff onto the roof for the flag-raising and -lowering. *Old Faithful; 307/344–7311 or 866/439–7375; www.travelyellowstone.com.* **$$$–$$$$**

Old Faithful Snow Lodge Cabins. Both varieties of Snow Lodge cabins have a clean, motel-style look, with plain wood furniture and some nonthreatening landscape art hanging on the walls. The four-plex Western cabins are a little larger and brighter, with wood-and-shingle exteriors and very small porches. The duplex Frontier cabins are a bit plainer. The cabin cluster is tucked behind the developed area around the Snow Lodge, with a less-than-inspiring view of the village access road. Expect to walk a quarter-mile or so to shopping and dining at the lodge or general store. *Old Faithful; 307/344-7311 or 866/439-7375; www.travelyellowstone.com.* **$$$**

Old Faithful Lodge Cabins. Though this complex's 1928 lodge is a magnificent stone-and-wood structure looking out over the glistening jet of Old Faithful, the cabins themselves are more dated than historic. Budget cabins look like tiny wooden utility sheds from the outside, share a bathroom complex, and sleep three in a double and single bed. Frontier cabins are a slight step up, with one or two doubles and private bathrooms. Cabins are packed pretty tight, but a handful are within earshot of the Firehole River, and you can't really beat the proximity to Old Faithful. *Old Faithful; 307/344-7311 or 866/439-7375; www.travelyellowstone.com.* **$$–$$$**

LAKE VILLAGE

★**LAKE YELLOWSTONE HOTEL.** Everything here is a peculiar shade of rosy salmon, from the walls, curtains, and comforters in the tiny but elegant guest rooms to the colonnades in the sunroom. It's like walking through the Mary Kay headquarters, but if you can learn to love the all-encompassing pinkness, this is one of Yellowstone's most refined and relaxed places to stay. The lake view and the tinkling of piano keys make it easy to lose an afternoon in the sunroom. The hotel

Lake Yellowstone Hotel was built plain and boxy in 1891; architect Robert Reamer spruced it up with columns in 1904.

YELLOWSTONE AND GRAND TETON NATIONAL PARKS

gift shop specializes in fine crystal, and the dining room is one of the park's best. Lake Yellowstone Hotel is the oldest Yellowstone structure still in use, though the photogenic front portico was added later. *Lake Village; 307/344–7311 or 866/439–7375; www.travel yellowstone.com.* **$$$–$$$$**

Lake Yellowstone Cabins. These garish yellow shacks clustered on an exposed lot behind the Lake Yellowstone Hotel were built in the 1920s, and they look their age from the outside. All were remodeled around 2004, though, and the interiors are actually spacious, clean, and modern, if bland. Each has a private bathroom and two double beds; the common areas of the Lake Yellowstone Hotel are a short walk away. Don't be surprised to open your front door and find a bison browsing nonchalantly on your lawn. *Lake Village; 307/344–7311 or 866/439–7375; www.travel yellowstone.com.* **$$$**

Lake Lodge Cabins. The Lake Lodge itself, a five-minute walk from the most distant cabin, is a pine-log masterpiece with a lounge and a porch that might be the two best places to unwind in all of Yellowstone. Like the lounge, the cabins date back to the 1920s, but they lack its rustic charm. Furnishings in the cheaper Pioneer cabins are quite dated, all wood paneling and aged carpeting. The multiunit Western cabins are similarly out of date, and light sleepers should beware the thin walls. Still, all the cabins have private bathrooms, plus a quiet, wooded setting with dining, laundry, and a gift shop just up the road in the lodge. *Lake Village; 307/344–7311 or 866/439–7375; www.travel yellowstone.com.* **$$–$$$**

THE FATHER OF PARKITECHTURE

Robert Reamer was just 29 when Yellowstone's first major concessionaire commissioned him for a new inn near the geyser basin at Old Faithful. Though a tremendous talent, the self-taught, transplanted Easterner was also a drinking man, and as one biographer wrote, he was rumored to have "sketched the plans while coming shakily out of a monumental submersion in malt." Reamer was also incredibly dedicated, often neglecting to eat or change clothes during the 1903–04 construction of the Old Faithful Inn.

The Arts and Crafts–style detailing in Reamer's inn, the use of materials to mimic the natural surroundings, and the building's scale all helped solidify a notion of national park architecture in the public consciousness. His approach handily bridged the gap between rustic and elegant. Reamer became Yellowstone's go-to architect for the next 35 years, renovating the hotels at Lake and Mammoth and building the Lake Lodge and the Prairie-style (and now demolished) Canyon Hotel. He also added the asymmetrical wings to his masterwork at Old Faithful and designed the Roosevelt Arch in the gateway town of Gardiner. We have his influential style to thank for every gaudy stone fireplace and faux-pine chandelier that finds its way into a motel in Greater Yellowstone.

GRANT VILLAGE

Grant Village Lodge. The six generic gray rectangles that make up the lodge at Grant aren't much to look at, inside or out, but they're clean and modern. The "front desk" is a small office building a short distance from the motel complex. Guest rooms have two double beds and private, albeit small, bathrooms. You might score a lake view if you book very early—the alternative is a parking lot. It's a two-minute walk through lodgepole forest to reach either of the village's restaurants. *Grant Village; 307/344–7311 or 866/439–7375; www.travelyellowstone. com.* $$$

YELLOWSTONE'S UPPER LOOP

MAMMOTH

★**MAMMOTH CABINS.** Though far from luxurious, Mammoth's clean, well-situated cabins are the best in the park. Take your average comfy-but-no-frills hotel room. Put it under its own roof, within sauntering distance of village amenities. Tack on a small, shaded porch. Add elk wandering by. A night in the Mammoth cabins is, on average, $10 cheaper than in the Mammoth Hot Springs Hotel, and what you lose in front-desk service and decorous common areas, you gain in that most underrated of amenities, the great outdoors. The simple units are virtually identical to the hotel's (right down to the option of private bathrooms versus shared), but you can spend an evening on your porch making eyes with a she-elk—and in four of the cabins you can do this from a hot tub. *Mammoth Hot Springs; 307/344–7311 or 866/439–7375; www.travelyellowstone.com.* $$–$$$

Mammoth Hot Springs Hotel. The public spaces outshine the rooms at the site of Yellowstone's first tourist accommodation. In the stately Map Room, dirt-stained hikers and bejeweled dowagers sit side by side, gazing out floor-to-ceiling windows at the antics of elk herds. Guest rooms come with or without bathrooms, and while both varieties are spartan, wood headboards and vanities keep them from being austere. In two available suites you'll find that rarest of all Yellowstone species, the cable television. *Mammoth Hot Springs; 307/344–7311 or 866/439–7375; www.travelyellowstone.com.* $$–$$$

ROOSEVELT

Horseback trail-riders from the Roosevelt Lodge, Yellowstone National Park.

Roosevelt Lodge. A dude ranch vibe dominates Roosevelt, where lanes between cabin rows have names like "Bronco Trail" and "Stampede Trail." The more economical Roughrider cabins have one to three double beds, shared bathrooms, and cast-iron wood-burning stoves.

The ostensibly nicer Frontier cabins are similarly decorated in plain wood and plaid but have two double beds, private bathrooms, and electric heat instead of stoves. The lodge itself is a giant, cozy cabin of rough-hewn timber and stone, with petrified wood incorporated into the foundation. Though the fireplace lobby works for a card game, the place to unwind is in a wooden rocking chair on the covered porch. Don't buy the myth that President Roosevelt camped here during his 1903 visit—Teddy's actual tent pad was up the road near Calcite Springs. *Roosevelt; 307/344-7311 or 866/439-7375; www.travelyellowstone.com.* **$$-$$$**

Stagecoach rides are part of the cowboy vibe at Yellowstone's Roosevelt Lodge.

CANYON

Cascade Lodge. This structure is part of "Canyon Lodge," the umbrella term for the lodging in this area. A reservation for a "lodge room" will get you a room in either Cascade or its neighbor, Dunraven Lodge. Pine furnishings nod at the sylvan setting, but both lodges are about as rustic as a set of plastic Lincoln logs—comfortable, but chain-motel drab. Cascade lacks both an elevator and a lobby. It's a 15-minute walk from either building to the front-desk building in the village square. Dining is similarly distant, but in a bustling location like Canyon, the relative isolation feels like a blessing. Keep an eye open for bison and elk lounging on Cascade's front lawn. *Canyon Village; 307/344–7311 or 866/439–7375; www.travel yellowstone.com.* **$$$**

Dunraven Lodge. Completed in 1999, Dunraven offers the atmosphere and comforts of a typical American budget chain. A well-kept exterior contrasts with the dated neighboring cabins, and the horizontal windows, stone detailing, and long, flat roofline mimic Yellowstone's more historic "parkitechture." An elevator glides between Dunraven's four floors, all rooms have full baths, and the lobby wouldn't look out of place at a Super 8. *Canyon Village; 307/344–7311 or 866/439–7375; www.travelyellowstone.com.* **$$$**

Canyon Cabins. These timber-frame cabins make up their own little village, three dense clusters of multiunit structures set in a wooded area behind the village square. The Western cabins are the best of the lot, with shaded porches and a bit of atmosphere in pine headboards, benches, and light fixtures. The Pioneer cabins are your budget option, sparse motel-style units with a simple decor that's straight out of 1950: beige carpeting, vinyl chairs, and a couple of faded buffalo prints hanging on once-white walls. Expect the same from the Frontier cabins, plus a few extra square feet. All have private bathrooms, with tubs in the Westerns. *Canyon Village; 307/344–7311 or 866/439–7375; www.travel yellowstone.com.* **$$–$$$**

MISSION ACCOMPLISHED?

As visitors streamed into the park following World War II, NPS officials launched a broad plan to upgrade Yellowstone's roads and guest facilities by 1966. The park's carrying capacity definitely grew under "Mission 66," but people have been known to decry the project's two biggest results, Canyon and Grant villages.

The boxy, modernist structures at Canyon opened in 1957, but the cabins and shops turned off a lot of park lodging diehards. Fans of the old Robert Reamer-designed Canyon Hotel continued to flock to it while the new rooms undersold. The grand hotel suffered from structural problems, but when it was demolished in 1959, some accused the NPS of a hidden agenda to make good on the Mission 66 cabin investment.

Grant Village represented a trade: a new development in exchange for removal of facilities at Fishing Bridge, a site that threatened critical grizzly habitat. But folks in Cody protested losing Fishing Bridge, which was their nearest village, and although park officials went forward with Grant, they drastically scaled back the Fishing Bridge removals. Then they further angered environmentalists by building Grant in a trout-spawning area about as important to grizzlies as the habitat they were trying to save. Tack on the village's maligned, nonrustic atmosphere and you see why Grant, for all its perks, is one of Yellowstone's most politically unpopular sites.

Grand Teton is even more
imposing in winter.

GRAND TETON NATIONAL PARK

Dornan's Spur Ranch Cabins. The Dornan's complex is like a miniature city, its sometimes frenzied set of shops and places to eat sitting just across the Snake River from park headquarters. Still, the pretty little cabins at Dornan's are set a few steps away from all that, gathered in a quiet cluster on the bank of the river, so you're more likely to spot a moose than a tourist with an antler hat. The cabins blend modern and rustic styles, with lodgepole furnishings and humble-looking wood exteriors but also carpeting, full refrigerators, and stoves. *Moose; 307-733-2522; www.dornans.com.* $$$$

Flagg Ranch Resort. During the early 1900s, Flagg Ranch evolved from a military station to a successful dude ranch, and a few of the log structures here are relics from those early days. The single-room cabins are modern, though, with private bathrooms and simple, motel-style furnishings. The wooded Rockefeller Parkway location makes for easy access to both Yellowstone and the Tetons. You can glimpse the Teton peaks from wooden rocking chairs on the small porches. There are lots of kids running around, as the ranch's rafting, horseback riding, and sightseeing tours attract families. *John D. Rockefeller Memorial Pkwy., 2 mi south of Yellowstone park boundary; 800/443-2311; www.flaggranch.com.* $$$$

Jackson Lake Lodge. This flat-roofed modernist castle centers around an expansive main hall, where guests unwind or plink on their laptops before a 60-foot viewing window overlooking Jackson Lake and Mount Moran. Surrounding the hall are multiple dining options, a lively bar, a gift shop, and an adventure desk that can set up lake cruises, horseback riding, and other activities. A few hundred cottage rooms laid out within walking distance are roomy with comfy but industrial furnishings and Native American–themed art on the walls. Rooms inside the lodge are mostly identical, but some have balconies and Teton views that will take your breath away. *Off U.S. 89/191/287, ½ mi north of Jackson Lake Junction; 307/543-3100 or 800/628-9988; www.gtlc.com.* $$$$

★JENNY LAKE LODGE. These small log cabins may be the handsomest lodging in all the national park system. From the luxe down comforters and handmade pine furnishings in the one-room cabins to the ornate hooked rugs and authentic wood-burning stoves in the suites, the trappings at Jenny Lake Lodge show a resortlike attention to detail. Also resortlike are the perks: free access to a fleet of shiny cruiser bikes, complimentary horseback rides, and meals in the knockout dining room. You can admire the Cathedral Group of

peaks from the main lodge's pine-log porch. *North Jenny Lake Loop; 307/543–3100 or 800/628–9988; www.gtlc.com.* **$$$$**

Signal Mountain Retreats. The mess of lodging choices at the bustling, lakefront Signal Mountain Lodge includes roomy bungalows, suite-style "lakeside retreats," and a monster, fully furnished log home. All three are a step up in comfort from the cabin options, with plush couches and small kitchens stocked with cookware. The log home sleeps up to six, and its gas fireplace and log interior give it a bit more ambience than the other options. The retreat rooms are the only units to take advantage of Signal Mountain's signature Teton views—Mount Moran practically invades your living room through a wide picture window. *Off Teton Park Rd., 3 mi south of Jackson Lake Junction; 307/543–2831 or 800/672–6012; www.signalmountainlodge. com.* **$$$$**

Triangle X Ranch. The last of the old dude ranches that once characterized Jackson Hole, Triangle X is a working stock ranch with a row of no-frills log cabins and a famously welcoming family atmosphere. The same family has been shoeing horses here since 1926, and though any stay revolves around the equestrian experience, ranch pursuits also include rafting and guided fly-fishing trips. Activities are included in the nightly rates, as are meals (thick steaks and other gut-busting Western fare served family style in the "big house"). On each cabin's open porch, Adirondack chairs face the mountains, perfect places to rest saddlesore backsides. *Triangle Ranch Road, off U.S. 89/26/191, 6 mi south of Moran Junction; 307/733–2183; www. trianglex.com.* **$$$$**

Signal Mountain Cabins. Although these rustic cabins lack a view, they're within a couple of minutes' walk of the Jackson Lake shoreline. Handmade pine chairs, tables, and bedposts add to the cabins' woodsy ambience. Blander, motel-style units are available, too. The varied floor plans sleep anywhere from two to six. Also a short walk away, the lodge itself is an unassuming stone and wood building with a lively television lounge always full of ebullient Europeans watching soccer matches. Search the lodge for the awesome full-size moose made entirely of scrap metal fragments, the work of a talented former employee. *Off Teton Park Rd., 3 mi south of Jackson Lake Junction; 307/543-2831 or 800/672-6012; www.signalmountainlodge.com.* **$$$-$$$$**

★**MOULTON RANCH CABINS.** From the porch of a century-old Jackson Hole homestead you can look across to arguably the park's finest view of the Teton Range. Photographers have been patronizing the old Moulton property for decades, in part to capture picturesque old farm structures like the nearby Moulton Barn, but also for the magnificent and unmarred view of the mountains. Five varied accommodations on this sunflower-dotted spread include the homestead's original bunkhouse as well as newer cabins. None is luxurious or particularly large, but the romance of country quilts and old barnwood is hard to resist. *Mormon Row, ½ mi south of Antelope Flats Rd.; 307/733-3749; www.moultonranchcabins.com.* **$$-$$$$**

Colter Bay Cabins. With some 200 cabins spread out across a mostly forested tract, the lodging complex at Colter Bay is like a bustling village. Not the place to contemplate nature in silence, but it's ideal if you want a bit of rusticity alongside cafés, shopping, and a launderette. The log structures have an authentic feel, with old-fashioned furniture and simple, patterned linens. Floor plans change from cabin to cabin; some have multiple rooms and most have a full bath. The cheaper, canvas-sided tent cabins are a cozy way to quasi-rough it, with bunked cots and shared bathrooms. *Off U.S. 89/191/287, 5 mi north of Jackson Lake Junction; 307/543-3100 or 800/628-9988; www. gtlc.com.* **Cabins $$-$$$$; tent cabins $**

Climber's Ranch. The American Alpine Club runs these humble shacks in the shadow of South Teton, open to climbers and their families (although technically, you don't have to be a club member to stay here). The former dude ranch offers dorm-style lodging only, and guests are responsible for bringing their own sleeping gear, linens, cookware, and pretty much everything else. Because the place is usually filled with charged-up rock hounds, the atmosphere is contagiously upbeat; this is a great place for climbers to make new friends. *Off Teton Park Rd., 4 mi north of Moose; 307/733–7271; www.american alpineclub.org.* $

JACKSON AREA

Alpine House. Are all the innkeepers in Jackson rock-star outdoorspeople? An Exum mountain guide and an Olympic biathlete are the gracious proprietors of Alpine House, a small inn with an eco-country flair near Town Square. Repurposed and recycled products are among the inn's building materials; local ingredients fill the menu; and energy use is wholly offset with purchased wind-power credits. In summer you can ride one of the inn's complimentary bikes. As you'd guess, the owners are great sources of advice on the outdoors. *285 North Glenwood St.; 307/739–1570; www.alpinehouse.com.* $$$$

Amangani. Perched atop East Gros Ventre Butte, the temple-like Amangani looks like it was built by some advanced but ancient civilization, all minimalist redwood walls, sandstone columns, and the scent of burning money. Floor-to-ceiling windows are everywhere, and it might be hard to tell whether you're indoors or out if it weren't for the bazillion thread-count linens, woven cowhide chairs, and plasma-screen TVs. Spa treatments and a heated outdoor infinity pool with a gobsmacking view round out the perks at Jackson's cushiest resort. *1535 N. East Butte Rd.; 307/734–7333; www.amanresorts. com.* $$$$

Snake River Lodge and Spa. A person sitting in the right spot in the Snake River Lodge lobby can count no fewer than six carved grizzly bear tchotchkes, plus one stuffed mountain lion. Don't let the Western bric-a-brac fool you, though—Snake River is all luxury. The stylish, contemporary rooms benefit from plush bedding and solid granite countertops; suites have views of slopes. It's a three-minute walk to the lifts, and beyond ski season you can entertain yourself with a whopping menu of spa treatments, concierge-planned activities of every type, and an indoor-outdoor pool area that looks like something from *The Blue Lagoon. 7710 Granite Loop Rd., Teton Village; 307/732–6000 or 800/975-7625; snakeriverlodge.rockresorts.com.* $$$$

★A TETON TREEHOUSE. Your hosts at this funky bed-and-breakfast are old Jackson Hole hands who can boast of a first ascent or two and are known around town for founding one of Jackson's first commercial rafting outfitters. You'll hear their stories around a breakfast table overflowing with homemade granola, freshly made breads, and other treats. The wooden bungalow isn't actually a treehouse, but it's atop a high hill, its wings winding among tree trunks. A lofty common area centers around an immense fireplace and a grand, wooden spiral staircase. Each room is unique, with a warm, lived-in feel. Some have decks and balconies that sprout at unpredictable angles. *6175 Heck of a Hill Rd., Wilson; 307/733–3233; www.cruising-america.com/tetontreehouse.* **$$$$**

Antler Inn. Budget lodging in Jackson is largely the domain of the chains, and often pushed out to the city's commercial hinterlands. Not so at the Antler, which offers motel-style lodging and a smattering of Western charm just a block from Town Square. From the building's old-timey wood facade and dated neon sign you might expect something a little chintzier, but the clean, simple rooms have nice touches like wood headboards and wireless access. *43 W. Pearl St.; 307/733–2535; www.townsquareinns.com/antler-inn.* **$$–$$$**

The Hostel X. Lodging in Teton Village tends to cater to the moneyed set, but if you're on a tighter budget, Hostel X has you covered. It's not truly a hostel, as the rooms are private, but it caters to ski and adventure bums who just want a bed, a bathroom, and a roof over their heads. A mellow fireplace lounge has some couches to flop on, a few board games, and a ski wax room. *3315 McCollister Dr.; 307/733–3415; www.hostelx.com.* **$$**

WEST YELLOWSTONE

Three Bear Lodge. A pine exterior gives this sprawling motel complex something of a country look, but inside, the rooms are standard modern. Unlike most West Yellowstone accommodations, Three Bears stays open through the off-season, catering to winter adventurers with snowcoach tours and snowmobile packages. Sled traffic on the streets surrounding the hotel can be pretty intense. The dim lounge has a cool collection of historic Yellowstone photos. *217 Yellowstone Ave.; 800/646–7353 or 406/646–7353; www.threebearlodge.com.* **$$–$$$**

The Historic Madison Hotel. The knotty-pine pillars and railings at the Madison are remnants of West Yellowstone's first days as a tourist town. The hotel itself was founded in 1912, and most rooms retain the historic feel with hand-carved headboards, pioneer-style quilts, and clawfoot tubs. There's a block of (less interesting) cabin-style motel rooms as well. Shared, dorm-style rooms upstairs make up West Yellowstone's only hostel. The on-site gift shop is so packed with tchotchkes you have to duck to avoid the dream catchers. *139 Yellowstone Ave.; 800/838–7745 or 406/646–7745; www.madisonhotelmotel.com.* **$–$$**

GARDINER

Yellowstone Village Inn. Wolf comforters, bison wallpaper, framed elk paintings...if you can print a tacky wildlife image on it, then they've got it at the Yellowstone Village Inn. The decorating may be over the top, but the rooms at this large, modern hotel are very clean and the staff appreciably sociable. Because the inn is on the northern outskirts of Gardiner, bison and elk have a tendency to loiter on the front lawn. *1102 Scott St.; 800/228–8158; www.yellowstonevinn.com.* **$$$**

Riverside Cottages. Nine simple cottages cluster in a small semicircle, making the most of a gravel parking lot in the middle of town. The property overlooks the Yellowstone River, and the units share a spacious deck with a roomy hot tub on the riverbank. A miniature pond and waterfall near the tub are home to the property's waterfowl mascots, including a goose that's a hit with younger guests. *521 W. Scott St.; 877/774–2836 or 406/848–7719; www.riversidecottages.com.* **$$–$$$**

⊕ CAMPGROUNDS

YELLOWSTONE'S LOWER LOOP

Madison Campground. Proximity is the major selling point at Madison. It's a short drive to West Yellowstone, a short drive to the geyser basins, and just a quick stroll to the wildlife-rich spread on the banks of the Madison River. A trail network winds from the campground down to the river meadow, where herds of elk and bison lounge year-round. Sites at Madison are tucked within thick pine stands and spread out enough that the area feels less congested than it is. There are flush toilets but no hookups or showers. *West Entrance Rd. at Madison Junction; 307/344–7311 or 866/439–7375; www.travelyellowstone.com.* **$**

YELLOWSTONE'S UPPER LOOP

Canyon Campground. Where a lot of campgrounds in Yellowstone could be taken at first glance for RV parks, Canyon is truly a camper's campground. About a third of the 272 sites are set aside for tents, and most are heavily wooded—great not just for shade, but for a semblance of privacy. Canyon's 7,700-foot elevation makes for chilly nights in early and late season. All sites are within a few minutes' walk of pay showers and laundry. Generators are permitted during the day at the RV sites. *Canyon Village; 307/344–7311 or 866/439–7375; www. travelyellowstone.com.* **$**

Indian Creek Campground. At just 75 sites, this comparatively small location is among a handful of Yellowstone frontcountry campgrounds with a decidedly backcountry feel. The sites themselves are clustered within a lodgepole forest, and it's just a quarter-mile walk up the adjacent Big Horn Pass Trail to reach meadows frequented by moose and elk. Two fairly mellow creeks flank the campground; Obsidian Creek to the east is a good place to fish for small brook trout. Adding to the wilderness ambience are vault toilets and the quiet that comes from banning generators. *Mammoth–Norris Road, 8 mi south of Mammoth; 307/344–7381; www.nps.gov/yell.* **$**

Tent campers at Indian Creek Campground in Yellowstone.

Pebble Creek Campground. Primitive, remote Pebble Creek is appealing for the ecological confrontations happening all around it, the transition zones where forest meets rock and rock meets water. The namesake creek runs through the wooded camp, and a half-mile walk upstream leads to a small, peaceful limestone canyon. Tent sites sit close enough for neighbors to hear each other, though they're set off from the smallish motorized sites. Big rigs should look elsewhere. This is grizzly country, so tent campers should utilize the food storage poles or risk an ecological confrontation of their own. *Northeast Entrance Road, 8 mi southwest of Northeast Entrance; 307/344–7381; www.nps.gov/yell.* **$**

Slough Creek Campground. You're in wild country at Slough Creek, where mule deer and bison wander right through camp and hordes of anglers relax after working the blue-ribbon trout stream. The first come, first served sites are decidedly primitive, providing only a picnic table, fire pit, and a few shared bear-proof storage con-

Pull back the
tent flaps for an
unparalleled view at
Grand Teton's Jenny
Lake Campground.

tainers. Half of the 29 sites can accommodate 30-foot RVs, while the rest are best suited to tents and smaller trailers. A few coveted sites sit directly on the creek. Listen at night for not-so-distant cries from the region's four wolf packs. *Slough Creek Road, 6 mi east of Tower Junction; 307/344–7381; www.nps.gov/yell.* **$**

GRAND TETON

Gros Ventre Campground. Gros Ventre Road sees a lot less traffic than the park's main thoroughfares, so you can still grab some peace and quiet at this campground, even though it's the park's largest. Though Gros Ventre tends not to fill up until late in the day, you should pull in early for your pick of sites. Some are on relatively exposed sagebrush prairie, others shaded by cottonwoods. Nightly ranger programs at the nearby amphitheater might focus on the bison you're almost guaranteed to see browsing the flats nearby. *Gros Ventre Rd., 5 mi northeast of U.S. 89/26/191; 307/543–3100 or 800/628–9988; www.gtlc.com.* **$**

 Lizard Creek Campground. More secluded and less developed than some of the monster campgrounds in Grand Teton, the sites at Lizard Creek are heavily wooded and right on the shore of Jackson Lake, making for killer views of the mountains. There are no showers, hookups, or staffed amenities at the first come, first served campground, but the toilets flush and there's drinking water on-site. Swimming and paddling are big here, except when low water occasionally turns the lakeside campsites into mud flats. It's worth calling to check on lake levels. *Off U.S. 89/191/287, 3 mi south of park boundary; 307/543–2831 or 800/672–6012; www.signalmountainlodge.com.* **$**

Grand Teton National Park Campgrounds at a Glance Chart

NAME	AREA	OPEN	RESERVATIONS	# OF SITES	FEE	RVs	FACILITIES
Colter Bay	Colter Bay Village	5/23–9/28	No	347	$18	Yes at most sites, generators permitted	Flush toilets, showers, laundry, marina, amphitheater, dump station
Colter Bay RV Park	Colter Bay Village	5/23–9/1	Yes (800/628–9988)	112	$35–$52	ALL, most sites pull-through, generators permitted	Flush toilets; water, sewer, and electrical hookups; amphitheater; showers; laundry; marina
Flagg Ranch	Rockefeller Parkway	5/23–9/21	Yes (800/443–2311)	171	$25/tent; $50/RV	97 sites, generators permitted	Flush toilets; showers; laundry; water, sewer, and electrical hookups
Gros Ventre	5 mi northeast of U.S. 89/26/191 on Gros Ventre Rd.	5/9–9/12	No	316	$18	Yes at most sites, generators permitted at some sites	Flush toilets, amphitheater, dump station
Jenny Lake	South Jenny Lake Junction	5/22-9/28	No	60	$19	No	Flush toilets
Lizard Creek	3 mi south of park boundary	6/6–9/2	No	60	$18	30 sites, generators permitted	Flush toilets
Signal Mountain	Signal Mountain Village	5/9–10/19	No	81	$18	75 sites, generators permitted	Flush toilets, boat launch, dump station, amphitheater

Yellowstone National Park Campgrounds at a Glance

NAME	AREA	OPEN	RESERVATIONS	# OF SITES	FEE	RVs	FACILITIES
Bridge Bay	2 mi southwest of Lake Village	5/23–9/14	Yes (800/439–7375)	431	$18.50	262 sites, generators permitted	Flush toilets, dump station, amphitheater, marina
Canyon	Canyon Village	6/6–9/7	Yes (800/439–7375)	272	$18.50	188 sites, generators permitted	Flush toilets, showers, laundry, dump station, amphitheater
Fishing Bridge RV Park	1.5 mi northeast of Lake Village	5/16–9/28	Yes (800/439–7375)	344	$36	All, generators permitted	Flush toilets; dumping station; amphitheater; showers; laundry; water, sewer, and electrical hookups
Grant	Grant Village	6/21–9/21	Yes (800/439–7375)	425	$18.50	256 sites, generators permitted	Flush toilets, dumping station, amphitheater, showers, laundry
Indian Creek	8 mi south of Mammoth	6/13–9/15	No	75	$12	All, 45 sites pull-through	Pit toilets
Lewis Lake	8 mi south of Grant Village	6/15–11/3	No	85	$12	All	Pit toilets, boat launch
Madison	Madison Junction	5/2–10/26	Yes (800/439–7375)	280	$18.50	149 sites, generators permitted	Flush toilets, dump station, amphitheater

Mammoth	Mammoth Village	Year-round	No	85	$14	All sites pull-through, generators permitted	Flush toilets, amphitheater, showers
Norris	Norris Junction	5/16–9/29	No	116	$14	All, generators permitted	Flush toilets, amphitheater
Pebble Creek	8 mi southwest of Northeast Entrance	6/13–9/29	No	36	$12	All	Pit toilets
Slough Creek	6 mi east of Tower Junction	5/23–10/31	No	29	$12	All	Pit toilets
Tower Fall	Tower–Roosevelt	5/16–9/29	No	32	$12	All	Pit toilets; amphitheater

Geology, Flora, and Fauna

Indian paintbrush is also called "prairie fire" for its bright, flamelike scarlet tufts.

An elk with antlers "in velvet." This fuzzy, skin-like layer circulates nutri-ents to growing antlers.

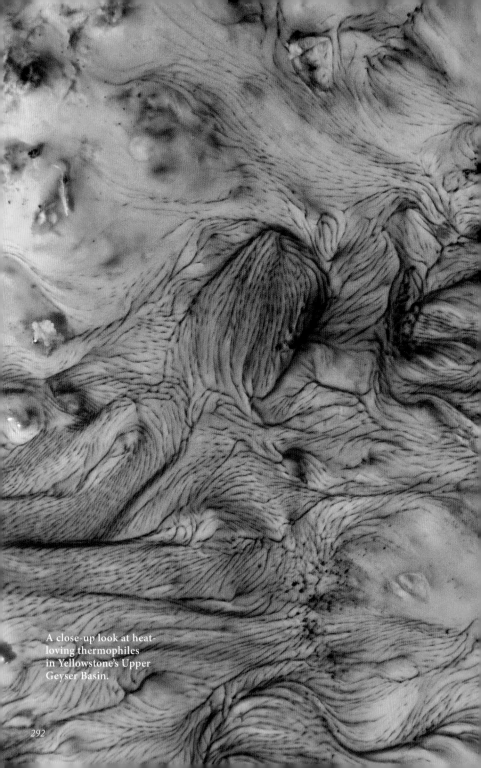

A close-up look at heat-loving thermophiles in Yellowstone's Upper Geyser Basin.

Such thermophiles create the namesake streaks of color at Orange Mound Spring in Yellowstone's Mammoth Hot Springs.

 **GEOLOGY**

Yellowstone's Hotspot

The first thing to remember is that we're all floating—all of us, all the time. We're adrift on huge continental islands or "plates" that comprise the planet's uppermost 50 to 80 miles, known to geologists as the lithosphere. These lithospheric plates drift around on a gurgling sea of plasticized rock called the asthenosphere, bumping and grinding and occasionally sliding beneath one another at a rate of an inch or two every year.

Another 1,500 miles below the asthenosphere, much deeper into the layer known as the lower mantle, the rock goes from plasticized to out-and-out molten. Gobs of this molten rock occasionally get so hot that they have to ascend—like the lava in a lava lamp—and they do so in long, narrow plumes running upward through the mantle. When these molten plumes hit the bottom of a solid lithospheric plate, they flatten out into the wide molten pools we call hotspots.

> Gobs of this molten rock occasionally get so hot that they have to ascend, like the lava in a lava lamp.

Yellowstone's hotspot formed between 20 and 70 million years ago, and many scientists believe its plume originates closer to the surface than those of other hotspots. What's certain is that the Yellowstone hotspot was originally farther west, in a way. As the continental plate crept slowly southwest over the plume, the hotspot left a traceable path through Oregon and Idaho in the remnants of magma chambers, places where molten rock from the hotspot rose up to the Earth's crust, pooled there, then erupted onto the surface.

Eruptions

The hotspot "arrived" beneath Yellowstone just over two million years ago, and wasted no time announcing its presence. A magma chamber just a few miles beneath the Earth's surface melted parts of the silica-rich crust, further filling itself with molten rhyolite and volcanic gases, amping up its own pressure. A little magma broke through the crust, triggering pressure-relieving earthquakes that caused the underground gases to instantaneously expand. The expansion of these gases forced magma, rock, and water vapor out from the chamber. This explosion, called the Huckleberry Ridge event, was so powerful that it left behind a 2,000-square-mile crater. Known as a caldera, the sinking crater swallowed up entire mountain ranges.

Similar volcanic blasts rocked the Yellowstone area twice since then. About 1.3 million years ago the Mesa Falls eruption left a smaller caldera just west of the current park, and 640,000 years ago the Lava Creek event created the 1,400-square-mile Yellowstone caldera we know today. This last explosion was roughly a thousand times bigger than the Mount St. Helens eruption in 1980; it created a cloud of ash that stretched from the Pacific Ocean to the Gulf of Mexico. Yellowstone's Mount Washburn and the cliffs at Gibbon Falls are both remnants of this caldera's rim.

There's still a magma chamber simmering beneath Yellowstone. Since the Lava Creek eruption, volcanic vents have released smaller rhyolite flows here and there, filling in parts of the caldera and smoothing it out to create the Yellowstone Plateau. The heat from the magma chamber powers the park's hydrothermal features (*see* the Spotlight On: Geothermal Features), and two "resurgent domes" have emerged at Sour Creek and Mallard Lake, where underground magma is rising to reinflate old, emptied chambers.

An eruption today on the scale of Lava Creek would cover half the country in ash, prompting catastrophic climate changes. But you shouldn't lose sleep over this disaster-movie scenario. The Yellowstone Volcano Observatory monitors what doomsday documentaries have dubbed the "Yellowstone Supervolcano," and they're not expecting another eruption anytime soon.

EARTHQUAKES AND THE TETON FAULT

The Absaroka Mountains were formed by intense volcanic activity some 45 to 55 million years ago, and afterward residual heat in the Earth's crust caused the North American Plate to stretch out, like pavement does during a hot summer. This stretching of the plates created faults in the Yellowstone area and these periodically act up, altering the park's hydrothermal plumbing (*see* the Gateway Towns chapter for more on the 1959 Hebgen Lake Earthquake).

The Teton Fault formed this way about 13 million years ago, as a crack running north to south along what's now the eastern front of the Teton Range. During millions of years of tremendous earthquakes—some prompted by energy from the hotspot—chunks of the eastern plate sank into the fault, sliding beneath and displacing chunks of the western plate. In essence, Jackson Hole has given rise to the mountains by pouring itself into the fault, thrusting rock upward from deep within the earth. As a result, the Tetons are the youngest mountains in the Rockies, but they're comprised of some of the oldest rocks. We have these seismic origins to thank for great views of the Tetons' sharp eastern face.

GLACIATION

Glaciers put the finishing touches on the modern Yellowstone and Grand Teton landscapes. During the last two million years, periods of cooling global temperatures sometimes caused great fields of snow and ice to build up in the Yellowstone high country, forming glaciers. In a process that repeated itself maybe a dozen times, these ice sheets advanced from the plateau into the surrounding country, then receded again as temperatures warmed. The most recent cycle, known as the Pinedale Glaciation, ended only 14,000 years ago. At its peak, the Pinedale ice sheet covered entire mountain ranges, smothering 10,000-foot peaks like a lead blanket over an X-ray patient.

As glaciers advanced and receded, they left evidence of their progress on the landscape. They broadened river valleys like the Madison and the Firehole, depositing debris swept down from higher elevations. Where glaciers melted rapidly, they dropped debris in great clumps, creating mounds like the Twin Buttes west of Midway Geyser Basin. In the Tetons, glaciers formed in the mountains, scooping out U-shaped canyons like huge, alpine half-pipes as they descended into Jackson Hole. As the glaciers reached into the valley, they pushed before them huge heaps of till (silt, clay, and gravel), piles that got left behind when the glaciers eventually receded. Known as moraines, these ridge-like piles trapped glacial meltwaters, forming Jenny Lake, Leigh Lake, and the other mirrored pools that sit at the foot of the Tetons.

FLORA

LODGEPOLE PINE

Lodgepole pine is the crabgrass of the arboreal world—it can grow anywhere, and it's impossible to get rid of. Yellowstone's ubiquitous stands of lofty, slender lodgepoles are superbly suited to the area's dry, inhospitable volcanic soil. What's more, some lodgepole cones require extreme temperatures to release their copious seeds, meaning lodgepoles actually benefit from the forest fires for which they provide fuel. The name derives from the Native Americans' use of the thin trunks to construct tepee frames.

WHERE THERE'S SMOKE

By the time the Yellowstone fires of 1988 were igniting, the NPS had spent roughly 15 years changing its fire-suppression policy in the park. But the resultant overabundance of fuel conspired with that summer's dry, windy conditions to scorch more than a third of the park. The gargantuan fires brought into public consciousness for the first time questions about fire's role in our dwindling natural heritage sites. Luckily, neighboring Grand Teton National Park escaped with minimal damage.

Fire is an essential component of the Yellowstone ecosystem. Among other things, it allows for plant succession, creates habitat, and restores soil nutrients. Purposefully set prescribed burns are more common in Grand Teton National Park than in Yellowstone, where high fuel loads near developed areas are usually cleared by hand, but the park does allow most natural fires to burn within preestablished limits. A fire set by a less-than-careful backpacker is suppressed, but fire from a lightning strike is likely only to be monitored, so long as weather conditions don't spell trouble and it doesn't threaten human life or property.

Current fire reports are posted in visitor centers and on each park's Web site.

QUAKING ASPEN

Often mistaken for birch because of its smooth white bark, the easily wind-trembled aspen has historically been more common in Grand Teton than Yellowstone. But ecologists theorize that a recent resurgence in Yellowstone's aspen can be traced to wolf reintroduction. The threat of wolf attacks keeps elk out of riparian zones on the northern range, places where they previously browsed on young aspen. In the elks' absence, the aspen's high branches have grown beyond the reach of the elk, greatly improving their chances of survival.

ENGELMANN SPRUCE

Engelmann spruce populates the Teton canyons above 6,800 feet, plus a few damp, high-elevation gullies throughout Yellowstone. Shallow, lateral roots allow the tree to get by on the thin alpine soils. The evergreen is one of the taller alpine trees, reaching between 40 and 130 feet at a mature age of 300 years. The spruce's blue-green needles are surprisingly sharp, so be careful brushing by.

GENTIAN

A number of different gentian species appear above 10,000 feet, all very small with thin, cup-like flowers. The prettiest is the fringed gentian, the official flower of Yellowstone National Park, which has lobes atop its ruffled, lavender cups. Arctic gentians have paler white cups spotted with purple. Both thrive in damp alpine bogs. The flowers are named for an ancient Balkan king who "discovered" their healing properties—not a discovery borne out by science, so please don't eat the gentians.

LUPINE

Bright blue thickets of this pro-
lific wildflower pop up all summer among lodgepole stands
and in sagebrush prairie.
Lupine flowers are legumes,
and the seeds are sometimes
used in cooking, but since parts
of the plant are poisonous it's
best not to taste.

INDIAN
PAINTBRUSH

Wyoming's state flower has eye-
catching, scarlet brushlike bracts
surrounding a small, yellowish
flower. Its other nickname is
"prairie fire," and when Indian
paintbrush blooms from mid-
June to September, the flowers
light up the meadows along the
Teton canyon trails. More than
a dozen different paintbrush
species occupy the parks. Each
filches water and nutrients from
the roots of surrounding plants.

FAUNA

TRUMPETER SWANS

Isolated trumpeter swan populations in
Yellowstone helped save this elegant waterfowl from extinction in the early 1900s.
Today, the continent's largest wild fowl
has bounced back nationwide, but populations in Greater Yellowstone are declining.
Migratory trumpeters are still a presence in
winter, though, and they show off a six- to
eight-foot wingspan when they land in the
unfrozen thermal-fed waters.

BISON

The nappy, dispassionate American bison may not be the park's most charismatic ungulate, but it's certainly the most iconic. Yellowstone's bison population dwindled to a mere 23 animals in 1902, but today, the country's only continuously wild herd numbers hovers around 4,000. A hefty bull can reach six feet at the shoulder and weigh a ton. Bulls and cows alike sport short, curved horns, which they'll use to gore tourists who invade their personal space—keep your distance! In winter, a bison's light-brown coat darkens and the animals grow noticeably wan as their diet of grasses and sedges becomes scarce. You'll hear "bison" and "buffalo" used interchangeably, but technically the latter refers to distant Asian and African relatives. The Lamar, Hayden, and Pelican valleys are among the most reliable places to spot bison herds throughout the year.

Bison and the Brucellosis Debate

Like many Yellowstone controversies, the current challenge facing bison involves balancing the needs of wildlife with the needs of ranchers. The ranching industry is on guard against brucellosis, a cattle-infecting disease that causes spontaneous abortion in cows. Yellowstone bison have been known to carry the bacteria since 1917, and they regularly migrate out of the park and into Montana in winter. Montana is currently certified as brucellosis-free, and it wants to stay that way.

Bison have never spread brucellosis to cattle, but the ranching industry isn't taking any chances. Because private cattle herds graze immediately outside Yellowstone in Montana, bison migrating out of the park are seen as a threat. A 2000 NPS manage-ment plan sought to prevent brucellosis from spreading while allowing bison some access outside the park, but components of the plan, like developing a vaccine and purchasing land for bison travel corridors, have had frustrating delays.

Without these measures, roaming bison are sometimes hazed back into Yellowstone, though most simply turn and walk out again. More often, they're sent to slaughterhouses by the NPS and Montana state agents. In the winter of 2007–2008, a record 1,500 wandering bison were sent to slaughter or legally shot by hunters, the overwhelming majority without being tested for brucellosis. Opponents like the Buffalo Field Campaign protest both the killings and the damage to the bison herd's genetic diversity.

WOLVES

Reintroduced in 1995, wolf packs now occupy every corner of Yellowstone and have extended into Grand Teton. At 70 to 120 pounds, grey wolves are larger than Yellowstone's coyotes and darker in color. They travel and hunt—mostly elk—in territorial, highly stratified packs led by an alpha male and female. Lamar Valley is typically a wolf-watching hotspot, especially in winter.

WOLF REINTRODUCTION: AN ECOLOGICAL CHAIN REACTION

The West's most maligned predator was a victim of systematic eradication from the moment settlers began showing up with livestock. By 1940, Yellowstone's wolves had been hunted, trapped, and poisoned out of existence. Reintroduction was first seriously proposed in the early 1970s, prompted by out-of-control elk populations and the passage of the Endangered Species Act.

After 20 years of intense back-and-forth with ranchers who feared livestock predation, the NPS transplanted 41 Canadian wolves into Yellowstone between 1995 and 1997. Ecologically, the process has largely been a smash. Today's wolf population fluctuates between 150 and 200 animals, with additional packs outside the park. Wolves helped cut elk numbers in half and subdued an unwieldy coyote population. Their presence is indirectly credited for the willow resurgence, which itself has been a boon to struggling beavers. Fewer coyotes, in turn, has meant higher survival rates among red foxes.

Controversy hasn't faded, though. Some critics insist wolves are now depleting elk herds on the northern range, though park biologists disagree. Other debates flared with the delisting of Wyoming's wolves in 2008, which permitted trophy hunting near the parks and a shoot-on-sight policy elsewhere in the state. Wolves regained protected status months later after a series of court battles.

BIGHORN SHEEP

Clambering along rocky ledges, bighorns fascinate with their ability to travel so easily where the rest of us can't. The docile herd animals, once central to Sheepeater diet and culture, were decimated by hunting and livestock diseases before 1900. They rebounded once protected from poachers. Rams have heavy, curled horns, while ewes' horns are short and slightly bent. You can often spot summering bighorns in the Gardner River Canyon, and during the early winter rut, listen for the thunder-crack of the 300-pound rams locking horns echoing in the canyons of the northern range.

EAGLES

Greater Yellowstone provides habitat for more than 100 breeding pairs of once-endangered bald eagles. These fish-eaters are readily spotted near water sources like Yellowstone Lake and the Madison and Snake rivers. Their broad nests top trees like over-sized, tangled crowns. Bald eagles' unmistakable white heads distinguish them from uniformly dark-brown golden eagles, which nest on cliffs and prey on small mammals.

BLACK BEARS

Black bears are sometimes cast as grizzlies' drowsy, likable cousins, but make no mistake: although the smaller foragers are largely vegetarians and more tolerant of humans, they can still be aggressive, especially if they're after food or protecting a cub. And they can still smell your freeze-dried dinner from a mile away. Black bears lack the grizzly's prominent shoulder hump, their ears are bigger, and their forehead-to-nose profile is straight. Most are indeed black, though tan or cinnamon-colored bears are not uncommon. Look for them in both parks' subalpine forests.

GRIZZLY BEARS

These furry bogeymen alternately fascinate and frighten. A mature male grizzly can weigh 700 pounds and stand 8 feet tall. Whitish shoulder hairs give grizzlies their name and help distinguish them from black bears, as do a distinctive muscle mass on their back and the convex curve of their snout. High meadows are their prime habitat, especially at dawn and dusk. Grand Teton has seen rising populations in recent decades, as Yellowstone bears migrate south. Hibernation generally lasts from around November to March, after which bears emerge hungry, prompting trail and campground closures.

ELK

Elk are the parks' most plentiful large mammals. Though populations vary (controversially!) each year, Greater Yellowstone supports around 100,000 of these regal herd animals. A bull's antlers can weigh 40 pounds and, in summer, shed a soft fur known as antler velvet. Elk congregate where forests meet meadows, summering at high elevations before migrating lower in winter— many to Jackson's National Elk Refuge. In September and October, bulls attract a "harem" of mating partners by bugling, a loud and surreal whistling.

MOUNTAIN LION

Chances are you won't see a mountain lion while visiting the parks, but that doesn't mean they're not out there. The stealthy, solitary cats, also called "cougars," establish territory in remote, rocky regions, though they may move to lower elevations in winter. They resemble tawny house cats, only 8 feet long and 150 pounds, able to take down a mule deer or elk. Attacks on humans are quite rare.

FLORA

ALPINE FORGET-ME-NOT

On these flower heads just a few millimeters across, a bright yellow center shines out from among five perfect sky-blue petals. These dainty-looking flowers are actually very hardy, adapted to the wind and poor soils of their high-elevation habitat by growing in low, broad mats. (They're only found above 10,000 feet.) They're Grand Teton National Park's official flower.

SUBALPINE FIR

The tops of subalpine firs point upward like evergreen dunce caps, narrow among the more blunted crowns of pines, Douglas firs, and spruces. Up close, you can identify a subalpine by the way its cones point upward on its higher branches. The trees love shade, so they can get a toehold in thick stands of lodgepoles and spruce. Crush a few of the flat, curved needles in your palm for a classic "Christmas-tree smell."

HUCKLEBERRY

Huckleberries are to Montana and Yellowstone what peaches are to Georgia. The tart little berries start as tiny white flowers, then grow purple and juicy on short shrubs in forested areas of south Yellowstone and Grand Teton. The berries ripen in mid-August. The lower reaches of the Teton are good places to hunt (but be sure of your identification before eating anything).

SAGEBRUSH

The ubiquitous gray-green shrubs found throughout the parks are the quintessential Western vegetation. Mule deer, sage grouse, and pronghorn browse the sagebrush's tiny, wedge-shaped leaves, although you'd find the taste bitter compared to conventional kitchen sage. The smell is similar, though, and after a rain, the sagebrush prairies of Lamar Valley and Jackson Hole are filled with the thick, sweet fragrance.

FAUNA

COYOTES

Imagine having food on your mind all the time. That's life for Yellowstone and Grand Teton's sniffing, fretting, foraging omnivore. Coyotes' indiscriminate diets include carrion, small mammals, insects, and grasses. Yellowstone's coyotes are husky, often thirty pounds or more, but their smaller size and distinctive, sulky trot distinguish them from much larger wolves. The gray-tan canines travel alone or in small packs and, with rare exceptions, pose little threat to humans.

MOOSE

Because the solitary moose feeds on fir, willows, and aspens, you're more likely to spot one in Grand Teton, where these trees are more abundant. Distinctive characteristics include the moose's antlers, flat like palmate satellite dishes. As tall as seven feet at the shoulder and pushing a thousand pounds, moose are formidable opponents with few natural predators. Spot them in marshy areas like Oxbow Bend around dawn and dusk.

CUTTHROAT TROUT

This native trout with a spotted tail is unique to the drainages of the Yellowstone and upper Snake rivers. The fish have lately faced stiff competition from lake trout introduced illegally. Lake trout devour the smaller cutthroats, sending cutthroat populations into freefall. (Yellowstone has a catch-and-release-only policy for cutthroats.) You can still watch leaping cutthroats at Fishing Bridge and LeHardy Rapids.

PIKA

These endangered, big-eared furballs are the size of small guinea pigs. Sometimes called rock rabbits, pikas (pronounced "pie-kas") live and graze on mountain-slope talus fields where rocks protect them from raptors and other predators.

Practical
Information

The Absaroka Mountains loom behind the Dubois Badlands,
just east of Grand Teton National Park.

⊶ BEST TIMES TO VISIT

A visit between mid-June and early September will give you the fullest access to both Yellowstone and Grand Teton national parks, and in general this is when you'll encounter the warmest, driest weather. These are the parks' busiest months by far. I think the best time to visit, though, is during the "shoulder seasons" of May through mid-June and mid-September through October. You'll brave colder temperatures, fewer concessionaire facilities, and maybe the occasional snowed-in road, but the rewards include relative solitude, better wildlife sightings, and the natural beauty of the transitional seasons. Ultimately, there is no "bad time" to visit, as every season in Greater Yellowstone does have something genuinely unique to offer.

Like grizzlies, the roads and facilities in Yellowstone begin to emerge from winter slumber in late April, and a **spring** visit reveals an ecosystem in renewal. You can feel nearly alone in the park this time of year, watching bison calves find their legs in early May or spotting antlerless elk returning from the winter ranges. The remains of animals that didn't make it through the winter and elk-calving in late May attract wolves and grizzlies to lower elevations, so wildlife-viewing is superb. Mountain runoff swells the waterfalls and rivers. You'll encounter snow here and there into June, so leave the sandals at home and expect occasional road closures.

Summer sees the peak number of visitors. Virtually all facilities open by mid-June and some 800,000 visitors appear in July alone, the park's busiest month. Sure, there are traffic jams, but there are also long days and warm nights made for hiking and camping. Carpets of wildflowers reach their vivid prime by July—earlier in the month at lower elevations, later as you ascend. The transformation of the sleepy gateway towns into bombastic tourism carnivals lasts until about September.

Seeking better forage, wildlife converges on the low county in **autumn,** so elk, bison, and moose seem as ubiquitous as lodgepoles throughout September and October. With a more diverse palette of trees, Grand Teton is especially scenic in early October, and squadrons of migrating waterfowl make pit stops on the many lakes. During the elk rut in September, their spine-tingling bugle calls echo across Jackson Hole and the Northern Range. The number of visitors in both parks tapers off in September and drops steeply in October.

Old Faithful gets more visitors in a single summer day than all of Yellowstone gets in January. And while year-round road access in

Grand Teton brings slightly more skiers and snowshoers into Jackson Hole, visiting either park in **winter** feels like stepping through the looking glass. Only the northernmost route through Yellowstone stays open to cars year-round, and hospitality concessions are sparse. *See* the Spotlight On: Winter in Greater Yellowstone for a detailed description of the parks' "quiet season."

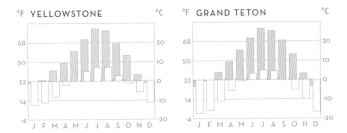

COMMUNICATIONS

PHONES

In both parks, pay phones are found in every developed area.

Cellular service with the nationwide carriers tends to be very reliable in the gateway towns of both Yellowstone and Grand Teton. Yellowstone itself has been cautiously and controversially installing cellular towers since 2001. As of this writing, plans to further increase coverage in the park are contingent upon continuing environmental assessments and are hotly debated. While supporters cite visitor expectations, public safety, and revenue, opponents argue that cell phones provide hikers with a false sense of security and that towers and chatter disrupt the wilderness experience.

At the time of this writing, Verizon Wireless and Alltel customers have strong reception in and around Mammoth, Old Faithful, Canyon, and Grant, with spotty reception reported around Lake. Users on other networks may occasionally encounter roaming access. Service in the backcountry, or anywhere away from major tourist centers, is basically nil.

Cell towers at Signal Mountain and the Jackson Hole Airport—combined with the valley's relative flatness—make cellular coverage quite thorough in Grand Teton National Park. Sprint, Verizon, and Alltel users will have luck at each of the lodges and campgrounds except Signal Mountain Lodge, where service is pretty spotty. There's also reliable reception along the two major roads and even occasionally along trails (useful for emergencies, not for gabbing while hiking). Roaming access on other networks is reliable.

INTERNET ACCESS

Wireless Internet access is readily available and usually free in all the gateway towns, where most hotels offer it (though you'll want to inquire) and cafés eagerly cater to digital junkies coming out of the park ready for their fix.

You won't find wireless Internet access in Yellowstone, nor do any lodges or cabins offer guest computers. Laptop users with cellular Internet cards should expect weak-to-no reception and slow speeds. About the only reliable Internet in the park is remote dial-up access in those rooms with telephones.

Grand Teton is another story. Wireless Internet signals are free, strong, and reliable in the lobbies at the Jackson Lake and Jenny Lake lodges, as well as in the lounge area at Signal Mountain and the bar at Dornan's Pizza & Pasta Company.

⊕ FESTIVALS AND SEASONAL EVENTS

SUMMER

(top) Pickin' and grinnin' at the Mountain Man rendezvous during Elkfest in Jackson; (bottom) a mess of antlers ready for auction at Elkfest.

Elkfest, Jackson. Come for the supermarketlike rows of thousands of elk antlers; stay for the live music, food, and historical reenactments. Jackson's most unique fest draws crowds to the Town Square to participate in the spectacle of the annual elk-antler auction (*see* "Bull Market" in the Gateway Towns chapter). *The weekend before Memorial Day Weekend; www.elkfest.org*

Jackson Hole Film Festival, Jackson. This annual juried flick fest rivals Sundance and other biggies for glitzy parties and celebrity sightings. Plus, both the modern Center for the Arts and WWII-era Teton Theater are gorgeous, classy venues. *Early June; www.jacksonholefilm festival.org*

Cody Stampede Rodeo, Cody. Much more than just burly cowpokes getting tossed off angry steers, the Stampede is one of the country's largest rodeo events: four days of parades, horse-and-rider acts, and more raucous country rock than in a Nashville honkytonk. *July 1–4, www.codystampederodeo.com*

Dog-sledding in the
Absaroka Mountains.

The annual torchlight parade at Snow King Resort lights up New Year's Eve.

Yellowstone Jazz Festival, Cody. Big band, swing, and instrumental jazz artists jam at the City Park band shell and other venues in the Rodeo Capital of the World. *Second weekend after July 4; www.tctwest. net/~yellowstonejazz*

Yellowstone Music Festival, Gardiner. An outdoor fest with a jam-packed stage in view of the Roosevelt Arch, Gardiner's bash brings in a lot of bluegrass and upbeat acoustic acts. The outdoor art fair incorporates some craft activities for kids, and there's a tent with local beer for grown-ups. *Sunday before Labor Day; www.yellowstone musicfest.com*

"Christmas" in Yellowstone, Yellowstone National Park. This longtime park employee tradition has become a favorite with guests, who drive north from Old Faithful to see Christmas Tree Rock, an island in the Firehole River with one spindly, garlanded lodgepole. Holiday meals and treats are served at Lake and Old Faithful, and if the staff has had their eggnog, you may even hear carolers. *August 25*

Winter

Yellowstone Ski Festival, West Yellowstone. A few weeks before snowmobiles take over the streets in West Yellowstone, thousands of cross-country skiers—from amateurs to Olympians—congregate for a week of races, clinics, and gear demonstrations. The carnival atmosphere carries into the town's bars and restaurants, many of which reopen just for the occasion. *Thanksgiving week; www.yellowstoneskifestival.com*

Jackson Hole Winter Carnival, Jackson. Galleries host special exhibits, bands play in the Town Square, and there's a parade and fireworks at the Snow King ski hill. The fest peaks when dozens of mushers and dog teams race through town, kicking off the annual International Pedigree Stage Stop Sled Dog Race. *The last weekend in January; www.jacksonholewintercarnival.com*

 **GETTING THERE**

By Air

Most major airlines serve Bozeman, Montana, and Jackson, Wyoming. Bozeman's **Gallatin Field** (406/388–8321) is 80 miles north of Gardiner via Paradise Valley and U.S. 89, or 90 miles north of West Yellowstone via Gallatin Canyon and U.S. 191. **Jackson Hole Airport** (307/733–7682) is inside Grand Teton National Park, 10 miles north of Jackson and about 50 miles south of Yellowstone's south entrance. Delta and

United serve Cody's **Yellowstone Regional Airport** (307/587–5096), 50 miles east of the park's east entrance along U.S. 20/40/16. From June through September, Delta affiliate SkyWest flies from Salt Lake City to the adorably small **Yellowstone Airport** in West Yellowstone, immediately outside the park. All four airports offer car rentals.

BY CAR

FROM BOZEMAN, MONTANA

The two-lane highways leading into Yellowstone from Bozeman are as scenic as anything inside the park. The Gallatin Canyon route, U.S. 191, to West Yellowstone is an occasionally cliff-hugging road following the Gallatin River—you may recognize the rugged Montana splendor from the film *A River Runs Through It*. On the other side of the Gallatins, U.S. 89 follows the Yellowstone River through Paradise Valley. Both routes can hug their respective rivers a little too close for comfort. Roadside wildlife is both a perk and a hazard. Despite Montana's reputation for lax speed limits, it is a pity and a peril to drive faster than what's posted (as low as 50 on U.S. 191, 70 on U.S. 89, both of which some locals consider too high). Lurching and speeding semis are also a danger, particularly in Gallatin Canyon. Best to avoid driving either route at night.

FROM CODY, WYOMING

Budget a good hour and a half for the stunning drive between Cody and Yellowstone's east entrance on U.S. 14/16/20, a two-lane road with the occasional passing lane. The last 28 miles before Yellowstone are designated as the **Buffalo Bill Cody Scenic Byway.** Steep cliffs and surreal rock formations overlook the road, which follows the thick blue braid of the North Fork of the Shoshone River. Still, this route tends to be less perilous than the highways from Bozeman, because it's not hugging the cliff faces, it's less steep, and it has fewer abrupt corners.

FROM SALT LAKE CITY, UTAH

It's a five-hour, 300-mile trip from the closest "big city," Salt Lake City, to either West Yellowstone or Jackson. The route follows Interstate 15 north for 170 miles to Pocatello, Idaho, where it enters the Snake River Plain. From Pocatello, the interstate swooshes northeast to Idaho Falls, where a series of U.S. highways leads either northeast to West Yellowstone or through Idaho's Big Hole Mountains and over the Teton Pass. Either route will put an RV's transmission to the test.

FROM BILLINGS, MONTANA

From the eastern Montana industrial center of Billings, it's 125 miles to tiny Cooke City and Yellowstone's northeast entrance. The route mostly follows U.S. 212, which becomes the astounding **Beartooth Scenic Highway** south of Red Lodge, Montana. The Northern Rockies' highest-elevation highway is breathtaking in summer and completely impassable the rest of the year—it's usually only open from Memorial Day until early October. The roller-coaster road leads through three national forests and past glinting glaciers in the Absaroka and Beartooth mountains. If you'd rather enter the park from the north or east, I–90 heads west from Billings to Livingston (115 miles) and Bozeman (140 miles).

GETTING INTO THE PARKS

Unless you're a super-dedicated cyclist or aboard a tour bus (*see* Guided Tours, *below*), a car is the only way to get into and explore Yellowstone and Grand Teton national parks. The entrance fee at either park is $25. This gives a single vehicle (and its occupants) seven-day access to both Yellowstone and Grand Teton. Put your admission receipt in your glove box—you'll need it for reentry. Motorcyclists save $5 on the fee, and folks on foot, bike, or skis pay $12. Entrance fees remain unchanged in the winter, though a $5 day permit is available for Grand Teton only. Standard entry can only be bought at the entrance stations.

Fifty dollars gets you a year's worth of unlimited access to both Yellowstone and Grand Teton, but if you're planning to visit more than two or three parks in a given year, the best value is an $80 America the Beautiful Pass. The wallet-sized plastic card covers entrance fees for a year at nearly every national park, plus a variety of national forests and other public lands. People over 62 get the same perks with the $10 lifetime Senior Pass, and a free lifetime Access Pass is available to those with disabilities. Any of these three special passes can be bought in advance at http://store.usgs.gov.

Passes are purchased at any of the parks' drive-through entrance stations. There are five such stations in Yellowstone. The **north entrance** is behind the Roosevelt Arch in Gardiner, Montana; the **west entrance** is in West Yellowstone, Montana; the quiet **northeast entrance** sits four miles west of Cooke City, Montana; 50 miles west of Cody, Wyoming, is the **east entrance;** and the **south entrance** separates Yellowstone from the Roosevelt Parkway along the South

Entrance Road. Grand Teton has only two entrance stations, both several miles inside the park's boundaries. The **southern station** is at Moose, where Moose–Wilson Road meets Teton Park Road. The **northern station** is at Moran Junction, where U.S. 287 joins U.S. 89.

For information on the visitor centers, *see* the regional chapters.

PETS IN THE PARKS

Pets are allowed into both parks, though they're barred from the backcountry, meaning you can have Fido with you only in the campground and around the villages. Pets in the backcountry risk spreading diseases to wildlife (or acquiring them), becoming lunch for bears or coyotes, and generally irritating other visitors. Make sure your pet is leashed at all times and never left tied out—rangers have very little patience with irresponsible pet owners. Every gateway town has kennels except West Yellowstone.

GETTING AROUND

Driving in Yellowstone

The figure-eight of Yellowstone's Grand Loop Road makes navigation in the park relatively simple. Nearly all of the most popular sights and boardwalk trails are found along this route. The five entrance roads simply meander between the entrance stations and corners of the two loop roads. On the pavement anyway, **it's hard to get lost in Yellowstone.**

Yellowstone National Park has a firm **45-mile-per-hour speed limit.** Obey it. Wildlife regularly sprints across the road, and behind every blind corner may be a herd of bison or elk nonchalantly straddling the center line. That RV in front of you will slam on its breaks without a moment's hesitation should the driver spot a bear in the neighboring meadow. Icy conditions can occur in high-elevation patches in the dead of summer. Neither Yellowstone nor Grand Teton is a place to take risks behind the wheel.

Anyone behind the wheel should make "patience is a virtue" a mantra. Traffic jams materialize and dissipate with the frequency and unpredictability of spring rains. When a herd of bison blocks your path in the road, you wait for them to move. It's their park, and **under no conditions should you attempt to disperse wildlife with your car.** Fellow drivers who neglect to use roadside pullouts can back up traffic for miles. The most you can do is keep your cool and resolve to

A male grizzly on
Mount Washburn,
in Yellowstone.

not be one of these inconsiderate sightseers. Use pullouts where provided, and if you must stop where they're not, maneuver as far to the side of the road as is prudent.

The park roads can slither up some steep grades, particularly going over Dunraven, Craig, and Sylvan passes. If you have doubts about your car or RV's ability to hack it, consult the map or talk with rangers about alternative routes. Should you find yourself in need of repairs, there are service stations at Old Faithful, Canyon, Grant, and Fishing Bridge. All have gas, as do additional stations at Mammoth and Roosevelt. In general, you'll pay a few cents more for petrol in the parks than you will in the gateway towns, which tend to have prices comparable to the those in the rest of Montana and Wyoming.

Road construction in Yellowstone is perpetual. The park newspapers provide updates on seasonal construction. For the most current information on **road conditions,** including construction info and openings/closings, call 307/344-2117. For road conditions outside the parks in either Wyoming or Montana, dial 511.

All Yellowstone **park roads close to cars** on November 3, except between the north and northeast entrance, which stays open year-round, and the Canyon–Tower Road over Dunraven Pass, which closes October 14 or earlier if snow makes it impassable. Snow accumulation permitting, Yellowstone's roads open to snowcoaches and snowmobiles on December 15, then close on a staggered schedule in early March.

Roads open in the spring on a complex schedule, beginning with those in the park's western half in mid-April and followed one at a time through May by the eastern routes. Park facilities open and close on an even more byzantine timetable—check the park's Web site or call 301/344-7381 for info.

DRIVING IN GRAND TETON

Grand Teton has a just few main roads, and all are clearly marked. The **speed limit is 45 miles per hour** in most places, although on U.S. 89/26/187 it occasionally goes up to 55 miles per hour. As in Yellowstone, **watch out for wildlife** crossing the roads—and be wary of other drivers who might brake suddenly. There are plenty of pullouts to use if you want to get a better look at something.

Inside Grand Teton, **gas** is sold at Colter Bay, Jackson Lake Lodge, Signal Mountain Lodge, and the Dornan's complex at Moose (you can also fill up at Flagg Ranch in the Parkway). Gas is a bit more expensive inside the park than in the gateway towns.

The spring **opening schedules for roads and facilities** are complex to say the least. It's best to check the park's Web site or call 307/739–3300 for schedules.

From November through April, Grand Teton bans motorized vehicles from most of Teton Park Road, the southern portion of Moose–Wilson Road, and Antelope Flats Road. Highway 89 remains open from Jackson to Flagg Ranch, though conditions may be snowy and icy—chains and all-season tires are recommended.

Road construction in Grand is sporadic. For the most current information on the park's **road conditions,** including construction info and openings/closings, call 307/738–3682.

Guided Tours

A host of operators lead bus trips through Yellowstone and Grand Teton from the surrounding towns. Scan the pamphlets at your hotel or just ask around—finding a scenic bus tour is probably one of the easiest things to do in Greater Yellowstone.

Among the most interesting tour operators are the park concessionaires themselves. In Yellowstone, **Xanterra** (307/344–7311 or 866/439–7375) operates a fleet of restored banana-colored buses. Each is from the early automobile era and looks like a stretch Rolls Royce (*see* the "Old Yeller Buses" sidebar in the Yellowstone's Lower Loop chapter). Half-day, full-day, and evening tours depart from every village in the park, exploring everything from the Old Faithful village roads to the rugged Beartooth Scenic Highway. Trips are priced from $12 to $90.

The **Grand Teton Lodge Company** (307/543–2100 or 800/628–9988) leads half-day or full-day Grand Teton tours with curator-guides who can spout impromptu bits of Jackson Hole history. Two-day excursions explore both parks. Tours range from $35 to $90 and leave from Jackson Lake Lodge or Colter Bay. Call for reservations or stop by the Jackson Lake Lodge activities desk or Colter Bay Marina. The company also runs a **free shuttle** three times a day between both sites and downtown Jackson.

Climbers hiking towards base camp in preparation for a Grand Teton ascent.

⊕⊷ LICENSES AND PERMITS

Boating

Privately owned boats—motorized and otherwise—require a permit purchased from either park. Weekly permits for motorized and non-

motorized boats are $20 and $10, respectively, and prices double for seasonal permits. Get one in Grand Teton at the Craig Thomas or Colter Bay visitor centers. In Yellowstone, permits are available at the south entrance, Bridge Bay ranger station, and Grant Village backcountry office, with nonmotorized permits also available at the west and northeast entrances, the Bechler ranger station, and the backcountry offices at Old Faithful, Canyon, and Mammoth. Open water is the name of the game, as the only river that allows paddlers is the Snake. Consult rangers to find out where else boats are prohibited and learn the precise rules for displaying your permit sticker.

FISHING

To fish in Yellowstone you need only a park-issued fishing permit, available at all ranger stations, visitor centers, and general stores. A three-day permit costs $15, a seven-day permit goes for $20, and a season permit costs $35. Kids under sixteen can get a free permit with an adult's signature.

Grand Teton anglers need a Wyoming fishing license, available at Signal Mountain and Colter Bay marinas and from Snake River Anglers in Moose. Non-resident annual licenses run more than $75, but day permits are available for just over $10 (license pricing is subject to change). Kids under fourteen can fish without a license.

With some exceptions, the fishing season in Yellowstone begins the Saturday of Memorial Day weekend and runs through the first Sunday in November. And, with some exceptions, lakes in Grand Teton are open year-round. Fishing rules in both parks are rife with exceptions, so it pays to listen to the rangers, ask a lot of questions, and get a copy of each park's regulations handbook. Identifying protected and exotic species is an especially necessary skill.

BACKPACKING

Both parks require that you have a permit to spend one or more nights in the backcountry. The permits reserve specific campsites for specific nights, so it's important to have your trip planned in detail when requesting one. It's also smart to have backup plans should your first-choice sites be taken.

Advance Yellowstone reservations are made by mail only (Backcountry Office, P.O. Box 168, Yellowstone National Park, WY 82190), beginning on April 1 for a $20 fee. In Grand Teton, permits for summer can be reserved for a $25 processing fee between January 1 and May 15, via mail (Backcountry Permits, P.O. Drawer 170,

Moose, WY 83012), fax (307/739–3443), or an online reservation system at https://backcountry.grandtetonpark.org/.

Pick up reserved permits from the Jenny Lake Ranger Station or Moose and Colter Bay visitor centers in Grand Teton and from virtually any ranger station or backcountry office in Yellowstone. Hikers can also request permits for free on a first-come-first-serve, walk-in basis, though in Yellowstone you can't do this more than 48 hours before your trip.

ONLINE RESOURCES

The **official NPS Web sites** for Yellowstone and Grand Teton are essential, if not always completely intuitive, clearinghouses for park information. *www.nps.gov/yell; www.nps.gov/grte*

Two NPS-produced Yellowstone video podcasts make for excellent primers on park history and biology. The **Inside Yellowstone podcasts** are two-minute overviews hosted by a ranger, usually covering specific locations and phenomena—a supplement to the park's interpretive signs. Episodes of *Yellowstone In-Depth* cover broader park topics in five- to ten-minute segments, mini-documentaries that might hold your teenager's interest on the drive in. *Available from iTunes or at www.nps.gov/yell/photosmultimedia*

The **Where the Buffalo Roam audio podcasts** put out by Teton Science Schools explore Jackson Hole's history and ecology. The 5- to 15-minute productions combine narration, interviews, field recordings, and music in the manner of a stylish public radio segment. *Available from iTunes or at www.tetonscience.org/blogs*

WolfQuest is an utterly addictive online game developed by the Minnesota Zoo, an educational tool that puts the player in control of a Yellowstone wolf, hunting, mating, and chasing coyotes across an astoundingly accurate digital representation of the park's Northern Range. *www.wolfquest.org*

The **"Backpacking 101"** feature from *Backpacker* magazine is a useful resource for those heading into the backcountry for the first time, a briefing on everything from basic first aid to quality trail-mix recipes. *www.backpacker.com/backpacking101*

Backpackers tackle the
Paintbrush Canyon Trail
in Grand Teton.

LEAVE NO TRACE

Leave No Trace principles are the law of the land in Yellowstone and Grand Teton. The "take only photos, leave only footprints" ethic applies in the frontcountry as well as in the backcountry. Below are a few basic tenets of Leave No Trace. Talk with rangers or visit www.lnt.org for a more detailed rundown.

- Pack out *everything* that you pack in— this includes all trash, leftover food, toilet paper, and other hygiene products.
- Minimize the impact of tents and campfires. Camp close together, and if you must have a fire, keep it small, using only dead and downed wood.
- Dispose of human waste properly by digging, then covering a six- to eight-inch hole, at least 200 yards from camp, trails, and water sources.
- Remove nothing from the parks in either the frontcountry or the backcountry. Don't pocket stones, don't pick wildflowers, don't take home that nifty elk antler you found near camp. Removing artifacts from the park is illegal, and rangers are far from lenient when it comes to this sort of vandalism.
- Never, under any circumstances, throw trash, rocks, or other debris into a thermal feature.

⊶ PARK PUBLICATIONS AND OTHER VISITOR INFO

Rangers at the entrance stations hand out maps and copies of the parks' newspapers. *Yellowstone Today* and *Teewinot* are published seasonally and print up-to-date lists of seasonal ranger programs, construction updates, and safety bulletins.

Short trail-guide pamphlets to Yellowstone's major boardwalk areas are available at each of the visitor centers for a 50¢ donation. You can also pick them up on the honor system at each of the trailheads. The Yellowstone Association runs impressively well-stocked bookstores at each of the park villages, plus at Madison, Norris, and West Thumb.

Worth picking up in Grand Teton are the pocket-sized guidebooks published by the Grand Teton Natural History Association. These volumes are concise but impressively researched introductions to the park's history, plant and animal life, geology, and waterways.

The chambers of commerce and tourist bureaus in the gateway towns are never short on literature of the pamphlet variety.

Cody Country Chamber of Commerce: 836 Sheridan Ave., Cody, WY; 307/587–2777; www.codychamber.org

Cooke City/Colter Pass/Silver Gate Chamber of Commerce: 205 Main St., Cooke City, MT; 406/838–2495; www.cookecitychamber.org

Gardiner Chamber of Commerce: 222 Park St., Gardiner, MT; 406/848–7971; www.gardinerchamber.com

Jackson Hole Central Reservations: 307/838–6606; www.jacksonholewy.com

Jackson Hole & Greater Yellowstone Visitor Center: 532 N. Cache St., Jackson, WY; 307/733–3316; www.jacksonholechamber.com

Park County Travel Council: 307/587–2297; www.pctc.org

West Yellowstone Chamber of Commerce: 211 Yellowstone Ave., West Yellowstone, MT; 406/646–7701; www.westyellowstonechamber.com

Yellowstone Country Tourism Region: 406/556–8680; www.yellowstonecountry.net

 SAFETY

It can't be overstated: Yellowstone and Grand Teton national parks can be dangerous places, and your safety is never guaranteed. A little caution and a little education go a long way, though. In addition to the tips below, remember to **stay cautious and alert around thermal features.** Don't leave the boardwalks in areas where they're provided, keep an eye on kids, never bring pets into thermal areas, and never try to touch or swim in a hot spring.

Rubbernecking causes car accidents far too often in both parks. When you just have to stop the car to snap that elk herd, be sure to use the pullouts or, at the very least, signal and pull as far onto the road's shoulder as possible.

HEALTH ISSUES

Giardia is a rather awful, though rarely fatal, condition caused by a parasite occasionally found in untreated drinking water. Giardia parasites travel in the fecal matter of animals like deer, sheep, and beavers (leading to the condition's nickname "beaver fever"), and are most commonly passed on via tainted food and water. Symptoms include explosive diarrhea, stomach pain, and nausea that can last six weeks untreated. Avoid giardia by treating your water in the backcountry, either by boiling it or preferably with a reliable commercial water filter. If you begin showing symptoms (which can manifest themselves weeks later), seek treatment from a doctor.

Visitors to Greater Yellowstone from lower elevations should be conscious of **altitude sickness.** Mild cases are not uncommon in mountain visitors, and symptoms include headaches, dizziness, and fatigue—similar to a hangover. Avoid it by drinking plenty of water and, if possible, spending a night or two at moderate elevations (say, 6,200 feet at Mammoth) before heading to higher ones (say, 7,800 feet at Lake). Severe cases are generally limited to high-elevation hikers and climbers, who risk fluid in the lungs and swelling of the brain by ascending too high too fast.

Hypothermia is always a danger to hikers, particularly in cold, wet weather. Shivering, slurred speech, and drowsiness are all symptoms of this potentially fatal condition. Prevent hypothermia by dressing appropriately for the Yellowstone climate. Wear a hat, avoid cotton materials that easily soak up water, and dress in layers, preferably with a windbreak layer. Boaters and paddlers in the parks' cold lakes face a particular risk, and should consider wearing a wetsuit. Severe hypothermia, characterized by disorientation, rigid muscles, and a slow pulse, requires evacuation and medical attention. But mild to moderate hypothermia can be treated in the field by sheltering, drying, and slowly warming the victim, most effectively with hot fluids and shared body heat. A hypothermia victim needs an increase in core warmth, not surface warmth, so rubbing the skin is ineffective and can even be dangerous.

The rodent-carried **hantavirus** has been responsible for a dozen or so human deaths in Wyoming and Montana since the early 1990s. The respiratory disease is most often contracted by handling or inhaling particles of urine, feces, and saliva from infected deer mice. It's a serious condition that can be fatal. Store food in rodent-proof containers, and camp away from potential mouse burrows like wood piles. Absolutely avoid contact with mouse droppings, which look like black or dark brown grains of rice. Should you encounter any in a room or cabin, leave immediately and notify the staff. Should you come down with flulike symptoms following potential exposure, seek medial attention immediately.

Though **ticks** are common in Yellowstone—particularly in the high grass of the prairies—tick-borne diseases like Lyme Disease are very rarely reported. Still, it's good to take precautions. Avoid loose clothing. Tuck your shirt into your pants and your pants into your boots. Wear an insect repellent containing DEET and check your clothes and skin thoroughly after hiking. Remove any ticks promptly, pulling them straight up from as close to the skin as possible, preferably with blunt tweezers or forceps. Apply antiseptic ointment to the area, and inspect to see whether any mouthparts were left in the skin. If they were, or if you begin to show a rash or run a fever, see a doctor.

The long, thrilling howl of wolves often echoes around parts of Yellowstone and Grand Teton.

WILDLIFE

Hiking and camping in bear country present unique dangers that can be minimized with some preparation. For starters, **don't hike alone.** Make noise when approaching blind corners and dense underbrush. Bear bells aren't all that effective, and, frankly, they're a little goofy. An occasional shout will do the trick—I'm a trail singer, myself. Avoid hiking after dark at all costs, and consider carrying a cayenne-based bear spray, available at the general stores.

Don't leave food out at camp and never store food in your tent, either in the frontcountry or the backcountry. Bears have a superpowerful sense of smell, and they can smell food from literally miles away. At backcountry campsites in particular, use common sense in food preparation and storage. Store and prepare food downwind from your campsite, and don't wear to bed the same clothes you cooked in. Use a bear-proof storage container (mandatory and supplied in Grand Teton) or bundle and tie your food to the bear poles provided at most Yellowstone backcountry campsites.

Watch for signs—tracks and droppings—and be willing to turn back rather than risk a confrontation. Never approach a bear in the frontcountry or the backcountry, and never feed a bear under any circumstances. A fed bear, as they say, is a dead bear, since the park service is forced to euthanize bears that lose their fear of humans. Though it sounds like a dull textbook, Stephen Herrero's *Bear Attacks: Their Causes and Avoidance* is an excellent intro to bear country, and it's available in the Yellowstone Association's bookstores.

Grizzly bear males are also known as boars.

If you spot a bear, be sure to give it at least 100 yards of clearance. If you encounter a bear at a closer distance, face it and back away slowly, making some noise or speaking firmly at a moderate volume. **Don't run,** which could trigger the bear's instinct to chase. Playing dead while protecting your head and neck is a last resort should the bear charge. Also remember, though cubs may look cuddly and harmless, mama is never far behind, and sows are fiercely protective of their cubs.

More park visitors are injured by bison and other animals each year than by bears. (Bison are unpredictable and not at all as docile as they look.) **Stay at least 25 yards away from other wildlife,** and at least 100 yards away from wolves.

RECOMMENDED BOOKS AND FILMS

BOOKS

Anderson, Roger and Carol Shively, *A Ranger's Guide to Yellowstone Day Hikes,* 2000. A hiking guide you can read for pleasure, this thin volume is rich with stories about Yellowstone's human and natural history.

Burt, Struthers, *Diary of a Dude Wrangler,* 1924. Burt's surprisingly heartfelt dude-ranching memoir dishes on Jackson's then-fledgling tourist trade. It's out of print, so look for this at libraries or used-book sellers.

Cahill, Tim, *Lost in My Own Backyard: A Walk in Yellowstone National Park,* 2004. One of our savviest travel writers dozes off next to feeding grizzlies and gets spooked by stone goblins while exploring and explaining the million-plus acres out his back door.

Haines, Aubrey, *The Yellowstone Story,* 1977. Yellowstone's definitive, two-volume history isn't always a page-turner, but you can be drawn in by sketches of oddball park characters and accounts of the fascinating backroom battles that shaped the park.

Peacock, Doug and Andrea, *The Essential Grizzly: The Mingled Fates of Men and Bears,* 2006. Taking a broad look at human/grizzly relations—the good, the bad, and the ugly—the authors argue that mankind benefits from occasionally abdicating the top of the food chain. Yellowstone's grizzlies in particular are a central part of the book.

Smith, Douglas W., and Gary Ferguson, *Decade of the Wolf: Returning the Wild to Yellowstone,* 2005. A biologist and a nature writer recap the drama that led to wolf reintroduction, and examine the cascading effects on Yellowstone's ecosystem ten years later.

Turner, Jack, *Teewinot* (2000) and *Travels in Greater Yellowstone* (2008). With the patience of a philosopher and the lyricism of a poet, climbing guide Turner examines, respectively, Teton climbing culture and the complexities of Yellowstone's ecosystems. Each is a deeply personal introduction to the area.

Whittlesey, Lee, *Death in Yellowstone: Accidents and Foolhardiness in the First National Park,* 1995. Who'd have thought we'd figure out so many ways to die inside 3,500 square miles? The park historian's morbid-but-fascinating catalog counts them down.

FILMS

Christmas in Yellowstone, 2006. Set to a lush orchestral score, this masterpiece collection of moving images captures the silent, snow-covered kingdom that is Yellowstone in winter.

In the Valley of the Wolves, 2007. This brilliantly shot documentary traces the rise and fall of Yellowstone's Druid wolf pack, with enough drama and spectacle to rival any Hollywood epic.

Index

The Teton range reflected in
a beaver pond, Grand Teton
National Park.

Acknowledgments

A grizzly bear by Yellowstone Lake.

⦿ FROM THE PUBLISHER

All photographs in this book are by Jeff Vanuga unless otherwise noted below. Compass American Guides is grateful to the following individuals or organizations for the use of photographs or illustrations:

Greater Yellowstone's History: 47 (both portraits), *Independence National Historic Park, Philadelphia.* 49 (left), *National Archives and Records Administration.* 49 (right), *Public Domain.* 50, 52, and 53, *Library of Congress Prints and Photographs Division.* 54 (top), *Colorado Historical Society, William Henry Jackson Collection.* 54 (bottom) and 55 (top), *National Park Service.* 55 (bottom), *Western History/Genealogy Dept., Denver Public Library.* 56, *National Park Service.* 58-59, *Library of Congress Prints and Photographs Division.*

Yellowstone's Lower Loop: 80, Sharon D./Shutterstock. 97 (left), *Ed Austin & Herb Jones/National Park Service.*

Yellowstone's Upper Loop: 153 (all), *Department of the Interior, Yellowstone National Park.* 160, *National Park Service.*

Grand Teton National Park: 213 (bottom) and 217, *National Park Service.*

Geology, Flora and Fauna: 310, *Walter Siegmund/wikipedia.org.* 312 (left), 313 (left) and 314 (3rd from top), *National Park Service.* 315 (top), *RG Johnsson/National Park Service.* 315 (2nd from top), *Richard Lake/National Park Service.* 315 (third from top), *Keri Thorp/National Park Service.* 315 (bottom), *Ragesoss/wikipedia.org.*

Yellowstone River in Hayden
Valley, with Mount Washburn
in the background.

ABOUT THE AUTHOR

A transplanted Midwesterner, **Brian Kevin** first discovered Yellowstone and Grand Teton national parks as a hitchhiking college student in 2001. As an avid backpacker, Brian has since explored the parks in every season, drawn by the infinite variety of the Yellowstone backcountry. He has perched atop Teton peaks, roamed the geyser basins, and even waited tables as a seasonal employee.

Brian covers adventure travel and the outdoors for *Outside* and Away.com and has written about books, music, and culture for publications like *Paste, Plenty,* and *High Country News.* He lives with his wife, Melissa, in Missoula, Montana.

ABOUT THE PHOTOGRAPHER

Jeff Vanuga lives in Dubois, Wyoming, and has photographed professionally for more than 25 years. His work has been published worldwide in magazines such as *National Geographic, National Geographic Traveler, Audubon, Field and Stream,* and *Outside.* Companies such as Ford and Patagonia have also used his photographs for advertising media. He has won several major photography awards, including first place in the BBC Wildlife Photographer of the Year and the National Wildlife competitions. He has also hosted TV shows on nature photography for the Outdoor Life channel and leads photography tours around the world for Joseph Van Os Photo Safaris and First Light Photographic Workshops.